5-8

Juanita Brooks

not
by bread
alone

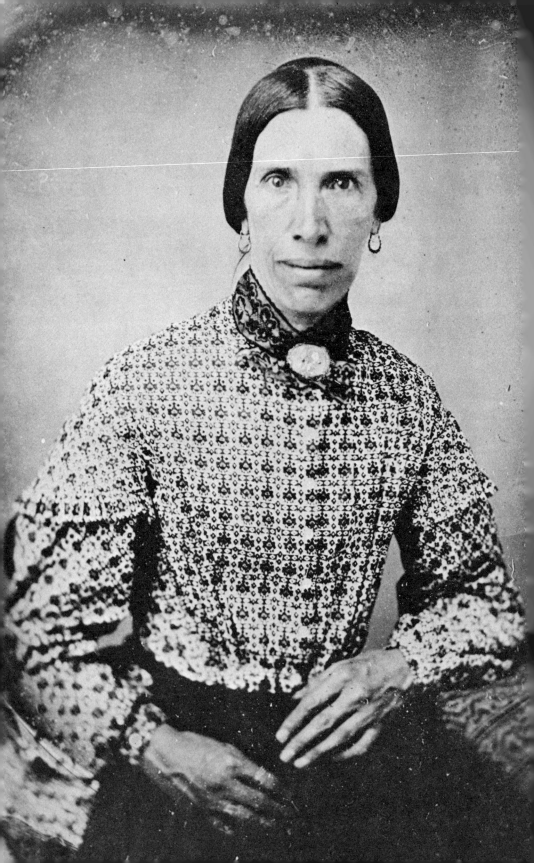

THE JOURNAL OF MARTHA SPENCE HEYWOOD
1850-56
EDITED BY JUANITA BROOKS

Utah State Historical Society
Salt Lake City

ACKNOWLEDGMENTS

To Yates Heywood for his cooperation and interest in the publication of this journal. To Miriam B. Murphy for considerable research that added to the depth and breadth of the footnotes. To Stanford J. Layton for supervising this project through numerous difficulties. To Laura Wells for volunteering many hours of proofreading.

CONTENTS

FRONTISPIECE: MARTHA SPENCE HEYWOOD

INTRODUCTION   1

1 TO ZION IN PEACE   7

2 THE LORD HAS LED ME ON   15

3 MY FEELINGS ARE SO CHILLED   26

4 A GOOD MAN BUT NOT INTERESTING   33

5 COMING INTO THE FAMILY   44

6 SOME INDICATIONS OF PREGNANCY   56

7 THE NEW SETTLEMENT OF SALT CREEK   64

8 LITTLE DIFFICULTIES   75

9 OPPOSITION TO MR. H.   91

10 ANOTHER LINK OF THE CHAIN   106

11 A NIGHT OF KEEN ANGUISH   116

12 ONCE MORE IN THE BOSOM OF
    MY HUSBAND'S FAMILY   124

    APPENDIX   133

    INDEX   136

Sunday January 5th 1851.

Last year, at this time, I was in Kanesville, living to
Brother Joseph & Johnston enjoying the prospect of coming
to this place having at that time heard such a glowing
description of it from the Brethren who came down there
from this place. The year before I was in Rochester, to
Mr Strongs, where my greatest enjoyment was derived
from the prospect I had of coming west. The year before
that I was living in Mr Hayes family. and I can call to
mind some circumstances of interest. I was not then
a mormon, nor had I made up my to become one
but just at that time Mr Heale returned from Philada
where he was baptized in the church & ordained an
Elder. He was delayed a week in Rochester on his
return to Canada and gave me his company every
day conversing on the subject of Mormonism. a short
time previous I received a letter from Mr White after
an omission of his correspondence for nearly two years
and also a letter from Mr Lewens. I was then surround
by advent friends & also some of my Baptist ones
especially Mrs Strong & her connexion.

The year before I was boarding to Mrs Gilson my mind
and was suffering very much with the disease of
my eye obliged to keep it bandaged up continually
The year before was to Mr Hayes on his farm at which
time I was in very low spirits on acct of my health
which was very poor at the time and the summer
The year before I was in the wilds of Canada West as
an advent preacher engaging the prospect of the coming
of the Saviour enduring the scoffs & privations that
attends such a course. Then I had not heard
the first lisp of Mormonism and thought there was
nothing ahead of the Saviours coming.
The year before I was in the city of New York living with
my father & step Mother & my sister Ellen lived near to
me very strong in the Advent faith to the annoyance of
her relations. My sister Anna Maria died the No
who lived in Brooklyn leaving her husband &
children to mourn her loss & those I occasionally
shortly before her death my brother Andrew
New York I had the pleasure of seeing him
sister Ellen & again in the street

Page from the Martha Spence Heywood journal. Courtesy of Yates Heywood.

INTRODUCTION

In the spring of 1933 the depression was at its deepest in southern Utah. For widows with young children and older people who were living alone the outlook was bleak. In St. George the LDS church began some "help each other" programs. Then the federal government's ERA (Emergency Relief Administration) plans were put into action by which people might earn as much as thirty dollars a month—a dollar a day—working on various projects.

Among the most significant of the ERA projects was one in which history was collected, written, and filed. Pioneer diaries and journals were copied and indexed; items from family histories and clippings from old newspapers were collected and preserved in suitable large books; the elderly were encouraged to tell their stories to women who would take them down in shorthand and transcribe them. Because I was then stake president of the LDS Relief Society and had done a little writing myself, I was put in charge of the project. At its peak some forty persons were involved in the collection of history.

One of the earliest acquisitions under this ERA program came through my friend Fay Ollerton who was gathering stories from ladies who had lived in polygamy. At Panguitch she received a box containing letters and a journal of Martha Spence for the years 1850 to 1856. Reading her journal was one of the most rewarding experiences of my life. Here was something special, something different.

In the intervening years, typescript copies of the journal at the Utah State Historical Society and other libraries were read by hundreds of students of Utah history, and it gained a reputation as one of the great pioneer Mormon diaries. Many plans were made for its publication, but questions arose concerning the location of the original. Not until the summer of 1975, after attending a Heywood family reunion, was I able to determine its whereabouts. Martha's journal is presently in the possession of Yates Heywood of Holbrook, Arizona, who has given his kind permission for its publication.

The typescript transcription has been used in preparing the book, and except for correcting obvious typographical errors (mostly transpositions), the printed journal reflects Martha's sometimes errant spellings and other peculiarities of her style.

From her first day on the road to Zion, Martha wrote vividly of many things: of the sick young man she had to tend in the back of the wagon, the teamster's language, the general nature of the terrain, and her joy when her friend Joseph E. Johnson spent more than an hour with her, and much more. Sometimes she worked back in time, sometimes her references are not quite clear. But for the most part it is a straightforward recording of the journey and her own reaction to the circumstances and the people around her.

Better still are Martha's accounts of living in Salt Lake City where she helped organize literary clubs, presented parts of *Hamlet,* called on the wives of the elite, attended church meetings and dances, and became the third wife of Joseph L. Heywood. Almost immediately her husband was called to settle Salt Creek. She went with him to the new town of Nephi on Salt Creek where she and the two children to be born of her marriage would live in a wagon box set off the running gears. Heywood's many duties separated him from Martha and their children for months at a time. The excitement of an official visit by Brigham Young or an occasional trip to Salt Lake City helped to ease her loneliness.

Martha's pen recorded many of the major events of the first decade of Utah settlement: the creation of Utah Territory and the naming of the first officials, including her husband as United States marshal; the colonization of many far-flung towns and the opening of Mormon missions in distant India and elsewhere; the public announcement of celestial marriage; the Walker War and the Gunnison Massacre; the building of the Old Tabernacle and the Beehive House and Lion House; and the threat of famine that sent settlers searching from town to town for grain.

More important perhaps than the recounting of well-known events are Martha's insights into Utah society. A candid diarist, she wrote of dissension in the ranks at Nephi (partly over her husband's leadership) and the loneliness of plural marriage with the same frankness she used to affirm her religious faith. Births, deaths, privation, uncertainty, joy, and hope filled her diary as they filled the lives of all the early settlers. Her story is different and memorable because she chose to tell it as fully and as honestly as her obvious intelligence allowed.

Martha included most of the important facts of her own life in the journal, and they need not be repeated here. Rather, for a proper perspective, it is necessary to introduce the leading male character, Joseph Leland Heywood. A son of Benjamin Heywood and Hannah Rawson, he was born August 1, 1815, in Grafton, Massachusetts. In his early years Joseph worked on his father's farm, but he soon decided that he preferred merchandising to farm work. At the age of twenty-four he went into partnership with a brother-in-law, Oliver Kimball, managing a store in Quincy, Illinois.

As a part of his work, Joseph traveled by boat on the Mississippi River. On one trip Miss Sarepta Marie Blodgett boarded the boat, and she was so beautiful that Joseph began courting her at once. Family lore says that his written proposal of marriage was a literary gem worthy of publication. The young couple married on June 25, 1841, when he was twenty-six years of age and she not quite twenty.

At the time of his marriage Heywood knew nothing of Mormonism, but in the fall of 1842 he visited Nauvoo and listened to the Prophet Joseph Smith preach. He was quickly converted and asked for baptism, although the stream was frozen along the bank. Orson Hyde performed the ceremony, while the prophet himself helped to cut the ice. Orson Hyde also confirmed him, assisted by the prophet and Jedediah M. Grant. A few years later Heywood managed the prophet's store in Nauvoo. Through all the troubles he remained active in defense of the church and its leaders.

When the exodus from Nauvoo began, Joseph Heywood was asked to remain with Almon W. Babbitt and John S. Fullmer to dispose of church property. It was a tense and perilous time during which several persons were killed and others wounded when the Mormons contended with angry mobs. The church agents managed the best they could, selling some properties and trading some for wagons and teams, grain, other supplies, oxen, and horned stock. They completed their work just in time to join the last train of the 1848 emigration from Winter Quarters.

The strain of this period was very hard on Joseph's young wife Sarepta, a delicate beauty who found frontier life difficult. A son was born who died almost immediately, and the 1850 Census listed one daughter, Alice, age three, at the Heywood home in Salt Lake City just north of the temple block. This remained the Heywood homestead until the death of Sarepta. In the spring of 1849 Heywood was appointed the first postmaster of Salt Lake City and soon after was set apart as bishop of the Seventeenth Ward, which position he would hold for six years.

Since merchandising was Heywood's business, he was sent with Edwin D. Woolley on a purchasing mission for the church to bring out some furniture, carpets, draperies, and other items needed to set up some homes and public buildings. He left Salt Lake City in the fall of 1849 and was not able to return until the fall of 1850 when he agreed to bring Martha Spence to Zion.

Martha's last journal entry was dated August 29, 1856. One can guess that her activities would continue much the same through the next few years: attending meetings, writing verses or essays to be read upon occasion, and making hats. Among the advertisements in the *Deseret News* during summer 1856 were the wares of harness makers, shoemakers, weavers, and tinsmiths, and assorted goods offered for sale, not for cash but for trade. Included was the Heywood advertisement:

HAT MANUFACTORY

The subscriber has established the above business on his premises in the 17th Ward, one block north of Temple Block, G.S.L. City, where he is prepared to execute orders for such qualities and styles as may be desired.

WANTED

in exchange for HATS—Otter, Beaver, Wolf, Musket, Fox, and Mink Pelts.
ALSO—Firewood, Butter, Eggs, Pork, Lard, Wheat, Lumber, Etc.

J. L. H.

Martha's skill at making hats and her teaching of it to others were being put to good use for the family.

When church authorities decided to plant settlements in the southern part of the territory for the purpose of raising cotton, ten families were called in early March 1857, and in April twenty-eight more were called to follow them. Although the mission was to raise cotton, they also had to raise enough wheat and vegetables to sustain themselves. Basic to all was water. This meant that at every spring of water a family or two would settle, plant gardens and small orchards, keep a few cows, pigs, and chickens, and manage to survive.

Early in 1861, 303 families were called to establish the city of St. George some five miles south of Washington, between the two red ridges through which the Santa Clara and the Virgin River ran. The families were selected to represent various trades and skills. Even a music leader was included, as were carpenters, bricklayers, tinsmiths, and cabinetmakers. Joseph L. Heywood's name was in its alphabetic place, listed as a hatter from the Seventeenth Ward.

Not all of the 303 whose names were called arrived at the campground at St. George. A few had stopped at one or another of the villages through which they had passed. Heywood stopped at Washington where several good adobe homes lay vacant. A. Karl Larson described the one taken over by Heywood as located "on the northwest corner of the Antone Neilson block on Highway 91."

Martha would really appreciate this home: its sturdy, thick adobe walls, solid lumber floor, and shingle roof meant that it would be warm in winter and cool in summer—quite different from the wagon box she had occupied for so many years. The living room with the large stone fireplace and its two glass windows were luxuries indeed. Martha had moved in and was ready to start a school before the new year. Her terms were high: three dollars a month, but this could be paid in produce of any kind. Some children hauled or carried fertilizer from their home corrals to spread on her garden; others helped to pull weeds or hoe on Saturdays; no child was denied attendance who really wanted to learn. Her skill as a teacher has become folklore in Dixie.

Martha was pleased that the Johnson family had come south also. Joseph E. had holdings at the Middleton Spring, halfway between St. George and Washington. Here Johnson experimented with plants and herbs. A gift from him of a beautiful pink oleander in a bucket became one of Martha's prized possessions.

Martha died on February 5, 1873. Her son, Neal, then twenty-two years of age, was still unmarried. Three years later he would marry a daughter of Prime T. Coleman, a long-time resident of Pinto.

What of Joseph Heywood and the other wives? Before the first move south, his fourth wife, Mary Bell, had two children, a son and

5

Joseph Leland Heywood.

Martha Spence Heywood and
her children, Sarepta Marie
and Joseph Neal.

a daughter, in addition to the Indian boy she had adopted earlier. This would have crowded the Salt Lake City home; so Heywood lost no time in moving Mary Bell to New Harmony. There, family genealogical records show, she had five additional children: a set of twins and three single births. Of these only two survived to maturity.

During the time Heywood lived in New Harmony, John D. Lee mentioned him several times as speaking at a funeral, reading the Declaration of Independence at a Fourth of July celebration, and serving on a committee for the Washington County Fair. In 1872 he moved his family to Panguitch where he lived out his life to age ninety-five. He died October 16, 1910. Mary Bell outlived him five years until September 5, 1915. In the meantime, Sarepta and Sister Vary (Sarah Symonds) had remained in the home at 45 West 200 North where Sarah died on February 6, 1881. Sarepta followed her on December 4, 1881.

Although each group has its own history and memories, the one permanent account is that of Martha Spence. This window into the past grows in value with the passing years.

JB

January 1st, 1850—Kanesville[1]—I take my pen to record this first day of the present year, and take a retrospective glance of the previous portion of time since my embracing this Latter-day work and being baptized therein, which event took place in Hamilton, C. W. (Canada)[2] in the month of July, 1848, while there for the purpose of more fully investigating the subject of Mormonism and deciding thereon. To Mr. Thomas Lewens of that place am I principally indebted for the knowledge of the work, who received his knowledge from Mr. David White, then of Brantford, but essentially aided by John C. Hall who also received his first knowledge from Lewens, but wishing to have his mind decided he journeyed to Philadelphia and there was baptized and on his return baptized Lewens and by him was I baptized.

Immediately after I was baptized I conceived the necessity of being where the Church was and at once decided that I would get there as quickly as possible. I tarried in Hamilton a few weeks, not enjoying myself very well in my brother's house in Dundas where I was nominally visiting, I returned to Rochester to the house of Mr. Alvah Strong.

---

[1] Kanesville (now Council Bluffs), Iowa, named in honor of the Mormons' friend Thomas L. Kane, was the place where immigrants bound for Salt Lake City, and also California, gathered to form wagon trains for the westward trek.

[2] Hamilton, Ontario, Canada, lies northwest of Buffalo, New York, on Lake Ontario. Dundas, mentioned below as the home of Martha's brother, is west of Hamilton.

Mrs. Strong being aware of my object and its termination in visiting Canada, she was right glad to see me. I acquainted her with my determination of going West as soon as possible. She was very skeptical as to my eventually leaving but promised her individual aid and sympathy should I do so, and as a first step offered a home in her house to save board expenses, and there I stayed, with a few weeks exception when I boarded with a Mrs. Knapp where I had an opportunity of promulgating some principles of Mormonism. But next to Mrs. Strong and family, I felt most interested to present the subject to Mr. and Mrs. J. H. Hayes but almost failed, my feelings and interest for that being very weak, having made my home here for ten years and loving them and their children as though they were my own kindred. Next was Mrs. Hall, sister of Elder Heber C. Kimball and I have hope that she will ere long come into this work, as also all my friends will in due time. I spent a happy winter's season in the society of Mr. and Mrs. Strong and their family doing all that I was capable of to interest Mr. Strong in the work. I formed an acquaintance with three Mormons there, Mr. and Mrs. Sackett and Mr. Freeman Rogus.

In the latter part of January, or beginning of February [1849], an Elder C. Dana passed through Rochester on a mission with the lady and with them I made an arrangement to be ready to accompany them on their return and journey in their company as far as St. Louis, looking upon the opportunity as a signal providence of God in my favor.[3] During the winter I had many opportunities of contending for the faith once delivered to the Saints, with friends and acquaintances from time to time.

On the return of Elder Dana and lady I took my departure from Rochester and from all my friends and acquaintances on the 12th of April, 1849—to the Western World, to a people whom I knew not and who were everywhere spoken evil against but trusting in the God of Israel that knoweth the purity of my intentions and who has ever protected me from all the vicissitudes of my meanderings during life. I started with a light heart and spirits as buoyant as air. Via Buffalo by railroad and thence to Sandusky by steamboat "Ohio" and thence to Cincinnati by railroad and thence to St. Louis by steamer "Paris" on rivers Ohio and Mississippi and I parted with Mr. and Mrs. Dana, leaving [myself] completely amongst strangers. In that city I stayed eight days waiting for a steamboat bound for

[3] Charles R. Dana became a member of the first territorial legislature in 1851 as a councilman representing Weber County. See Edward W. Tullidge, *History of Salt Lake City* (Salt Lake City, 1886), p. 81.

the Bluffs. I started on the night of the 2nd of May in steamer "Mary" with about 240 Mormons, Capt. Jones' Welsh company being the greater portion, together with several English families.[4] Cholera broke out before we got fairly started and nearly all the passengers and boat crew were the subjects of the pestilential influence. We lost 58 by death and the remains were buried on the banks as we came along.[5]

We arrived at Council Point on the night of the 16th of May, making just 14 days travel. We landed the next day and what an appearance of country presented itself to my view. The first home I entered was [that of] Mr. Sackett (of Rochester) who invited me to his house to stay until I got otherwise provided for, which I accepted but did not remain as I was anxious to get some employment to earn my own living.

I spent about two weeks with Elder Benson and enjoyed the society of his lady very much.[6] I also spent a few days with Mrs. Joseph Young [7] and while there the chance of a school offered itself which I accepted and in a few days located myself in Springville and found myself presiding over an interesting group of juveniles of all ages and while in the capacity of school teacher I made some interesting acquaintances, especially Brother Houston. The sympathy and hospitality I experienced from them has made an impression not easily effaced.

Since the termination of my school I have located myself here in Joseph E. Johnson's family for the purpose of making "Caps"

[4] The name of Dan Jones appears in many books on the western migration. Born August 4, 1811, in Flintshire, Wales, he had gained a college education before he came to America. In 1840 he owned a boat on the Mississippi River called *The Maid of Iowa*. He met Joseph Smith, Jr., and was converted to Mormonism, after which he used his boat for the benefit of the church. Jones was in the Carthage Jail the night before Joseph Smith's martyrdom. The prophet promised Jones that he would live to return to his native land and be the means of bringing many to Zion. In 1845 Dan Jones returned to Wales where in four years he baptized some two thousand persons and brought many of them to the West. See Andrew Jenson, *Latter-day Saint Biographical Encyclopedia*, 4 vols. (Salt Lake City: Andrew Jenson History Company, 1901–36), 3:658–60; Joseph Smith, Jr., *History of the Church of Jesus Christ of Latter-day Saints,* ed. Brigham H. Roberts, 7 vols. (Salt Lake City: Deseret News Press, 1902–32), 5:354.

[5] The worldwide cholera epidemic of 1840–62 killed millions.

[6] Ezra T. Benson had been named as an apostle in 1846. A member of the pioneer company of 1847, Benson left Salt Lake Valley late in 1847 "to preside in Pottawattamie county, Iowa, being associated with President Orson Hyde and George A. Smith." See Jenson, *LDS Biographical Encyclopedia*, 1:101.

[7] This was probably Jane Adeline Bicknell who married Joseph Young in 1834. Jenson, *LDS Biographical Encyclopedia,* 1:187.

but was disappointed in not getting materials.[8] I had an offer to go over to the Mission School from Mr. McKenna at two dollars a week with good home and would have accepted it but for having previously engaged my services to Mr. Johnson and the result was but little money making, but still I was amply repaid for this disappointment by having an opportunity of becoming well acquainted with Elder Taylor, Lorenzo and Erastus Snow and Franklin Richards going on missions to different nations of the earth and also many other of the brethren, their companions in the work.[9] Previous to the brethren's arrival I felt somewhat unhappy in mind as skepticism had crept in and opened the door to cavil at almost anything.

July[10]—Some weeks elapsed after the departure of the brethren before I lost that happy state of feeling, that they in the providence of God helped me to, and during the winter I felt most nervously anxious to go on to the valley in the spring—so much so that I said many times that I would walk there. I had two or three chances presented to me, but they signally failed but when feeling discouraged a hope would spring up in my mind that when Brothers Haywood and Woolley would return from the East,[11] that Brother Haywood would make a way for me to go, supposing he felt interested in having me go there for the purpose of making caps and also a faint hope that Mr. White would come along in the spring and make all things right, as also Mr. Lewens who had got as far as St. Louis, having received a letter from him in that place enclosing five dollars sent

[8] Joseph Ellis Johnson arrived in Kanesville in 1848 where he campaigned for a U. S. post office, built a home and a general store, and wrote for the *Frontier Guardian*. Martha may have anticipated selling her caps at Johnson's store. See Rufus David Johnson, *J.E.J., Trail to Sundown* ([Salt Lake City]: J. E. Johnson Family, 1961), pp. 105–11.

[9] At the October 1849 conference in Salt Lake City, John Taylor was called to go to France, Lorenzo Snow to Italy, Erastus Snow to Denmark, and Franklin D. Richards to England. Martha's memory of the men's arrival in Kanesville was probably sharpened by the reception accorded the elders who, according to Taylor, were "saluted with the firing of guns on our arrival, and the greatest manifestations of rejoicing, and parties, musical entertainments, etc. . . ." See Brigham H. Roberts, *The Life of John Taylor* (Salt Lake City, 1892), pp. 203, 207.

[10] Martha picked up her narrative after a lapse of seven months. She was writing in July 1850 about events of the winter of 1849–50.

[11] According to the *Frontier Guardian* (Kanesville, Ia.), May 29, 1850, Heywood had been in Washington where he visited President Zachary Taylor who received him cordially. At the conclusion of the interview, Heywood called on the president "to be a father to our people." Taylor reportedly replied, "I will try to do you all the good I can, and as little harm as possible." Taylor, as a major general in the Mexican War, was aware of the support the Mormons had given to that war through the Mormon Battalion. Unfortunately, Taylor died in office on July 9, 1850.

me in that by Mr. White.[12] About the same time I received a remembrance from Mrs. Strong enclosed in a very kind and affectionate letter. But my mind fell into an uncomfortable anxious state partly owing to the conflicting emotion occasioned by my several expectancies giving me an unsettled state of mind and purpose in all my actions. But amidst all this the kindness of Mr. Johnson showed as a bright star over the general opaque of my daily movements. His kindness was that of a beloved brother and [a] more congenial spirit in intellectual taste and refinement I have rarely met with, and my prayers shall be that he may yet be all that is noble and great in the kingdom and have congenial spirits around him.

My prospects of going to the Valley grew darker as time wore on. Brother Stevens of Springville gave up the hope of going. Joseph Young failed in the saw-mill [he] operated. I offered my services to a Mrs. Whitesides to do her work on the way, but she had to give up going, but yet other faint hopes raised my spirits at times for it was a hard stint with me to think that I could not go eventually. But time wore on and expectancy grew dimmer. About the middle of ———— I had word from Brother Haywood to prepare for going as he thought it possible he could get me along. This was a very great relief to my mind and lasted till he came up to Kanesville and threw out doubts of my going. About this time Mr. Lewens came along and was so disappointed in his cattle arrangements that he had to dispose of one of his wagons so that it was impossible to think of taking me; nor did I glean anything very satisfactory as to Mr. White excepting that he would certainly start this spring for the West.

Well, every chance failed—even Brother Haywood called for the last time to tell me he could not see his way clear enough to say I could go. That call decided me as to my remaining in Kanesville and I determined to locate myself comfortably for the coming year and perhaps for many years, not feeling disposed to make so thorough an exertion again to go to the Valley. I proposed to start me a select school and commenced boarding with Mr. Johnson's mother and went to some labor in preparing to live there, when at the end of another week Brother [Heywood?] called again to tell me I could go. I had my mind so settled as to there being a providence in my not going that I really felt disappointed in his telling me I could go but my own rule of action bound me to as I considered it equally a providence in his asking me to go.

[12] This may have been New Yorker Samuel Dennis White, a pioneer of 1850, whom Martha may have met when she was in Rochester.

At Bethlehem camp [13] we remained two weeks after I joined the company and on Sunday, June 30th, we crossed the river, having commenced on the Saturday. Monday we did not travel as the cattle had not been got over and there was no crossing that day. Tuesday traveled a mile or two and Wednesday the same. Thursday—Fourth of July—camped all day; washed, cooked and prepared the cattle for a real start on the following day. Friday we took the start, having to leave behind us a splendid ox who became diseased from some cause and could not travel—also a mare belonging to Brother Woolley [14] had a hurt in his leg and could not travel. We traveled twelve miles this day and camped with Brother Hunter's company [15] and made a corral of about 70 wagons, a new and pretty sight to me. Saturday we halted the forenoon during which time Elder Hyde and Brother Johnson overtook us but to our great surprise and disappointment did not take Brother Haywood with them as had been agreed up in Kanesville.[16] We have travelled nicely day after day up to this Wednesday—July 10th.

This morning the first sound that met our ears was the cry that the cattle were all gone. The mesquitoes were very bad indeed

[13] The travelers were still in Iowa, not having crossed the Missouri into Nebraska.

[14] Edwin Dilworth Woolley was sent east with Edward Hunter in 1849 to aid the emigration and to buy goods for the church. Later, Woolley succeeded Hunter as bishop of the Thirteenth Ward in Salt Lake City. See Jenson, *LDS Biographical Encyclopedia*, 1:632–33.

[15] Edward Hunter was sent by the First Presidency to the Missouri River in the fall of 1849 to supervise the emigration of the Saints. He took $5,000 to "set in motion the vast emigrating enterprise" [Perpetual Emigration Fund]. His was the last company to reach Salt Lake City in 1850. Later, Hunter became presiding bishop of the LDS church. Hunter's company was organized at Council Bluffs, Iowa, on July 4, 1850. It consisted of 261 emigrants. Joseph L. Heywood was named counselor to Hunter and Edwin D. Woolley captain. There were also seven captains of ten. In addition to persons and livestock, this company carried 4,877 pounds of freight from England to Salt Lake. See Jenson, *LDS Biographical Encyclopedia*, 1:227–32, and William E. Hunter, *Edward Hunter: Faithful Steward* (Salt Lake City: Mrs. W. E. Hunter, 1970), pp. 108–27.

[16] Orson Hyde, apostle and editor of the *Frontier Guardian*, set out on his first visit to Salt Lake Valley in July 1850. He was accompanied by Joseph E. Johnson, Kanesville merchant and friend of Martha Spence Heywood; Henry W. Miller, the first settler of Kanesville (earlier called Miller's Hollow), and Joseph Kelley. Evidently Joseph L. Heywood had planned to join the four men and make the trip to Salt Lake Valley with them. The four made good time crossing the plains and passed several companies, arriving in Salt Lake in mid-August. Johnson left the valley for Kanesville on September 30, 1850. The return company included Hyde, Miller, and Kelley, plus Capt. John Brown. They were greeted on their return by the citizens of Kanesville with cannon fire, banners, etc., in December 1850. Almost immediately after his return to Kanesville Johnson entered into polygamy, marrying Hannah Maria Goddard. Family members speculate that his hurried trip to Salt Lake was motivated by his desire to get approval for this plural marriage. See Johnson, *Trail to Sundown*, pp. 112–48.

which, no doubt, occasioned the cattle to stray, as also brother Haywood's horse. The cattle were found but not the horse. Brother Haywood had spent all day trying to find him but in all probability he has been stolen.

I have just had the melancholy intelligence that amongst the many who have died of cholera, Sister Margaret MacDougal and Sister Dana are reckoned among its victims. In those falling a victim I see the pestilence nearer to me than before and the question comes up in my mind, Who am I? that I may not be called upon. But Oh!, may my Heavenly Father avert the blow and spare my life a little longer. My desire is to live and glorify His name in doing the work he assigns me.

July 26th—Started this morning from Fort Kearny [17] after a stay of two days during which time we made some changes in our affairs for the better by lightening the wagons and dispensing with one, hereby strengthening some of the other teams and also procuring two additional yokes. Had a sale of crockery ware which seemed a pity as it was brought all the ways from Boston expressly for the benefit of those in the valley who had long been deprived of its convenience. And now we have a prospect of traveling more advantageously and although our traveling heretofore has been safe, comfortable and exempt from death or even sickness of any consequence. We had lost one yoke of cattle by getting into a hole with their yoke on and one or two others by giving out.

Col. Reese [18] and his train overtook us about one week from this date, bringing with them Brother Woolley's horse and news of Brother Haywood. It was seen, but would not be given, with a man in the United States Service, excusing himself from doing so by saying that he had orders to fetch him to Kanesville. We are daily seeing the mementos of the ravages of cholera. Sometimes three graves side by side. Another familiar name—Brother Sargeant of Kanesville —affected and aware of the severe and protracted sickness he passed through last summer and this spring previous to my leaving and at

[17] Fort Kearny was established in 1846 on the site of present Nebraska City. In 1848 it was relocated on the south bank of the Platte, some six miles southeast of present-day Kearney.

[18] The Reese brothers, John and Enoch, worked together closely in freighting and merchandising. In June 1851 the Reese brothers bought out the owner of a trading post in Carson Valley, Nevada. Later, John was excommunicated for refusing to accept the counsel of Apostle Orson Hyde over the matter of trying to collect bad debts from his non-Mormon customers. See Eugene E. Campbell, "Brigham Young's Outer Cordon—A Reappraisal," *Utah Historical Quarterly* 41 (1973): 236–39.

a time when my prospect for this journey looked rather gloomy he was all life and animation in getting his outfit and providing presents for his daughters in the Valley. It will be a heavy blow to his daughters in Kanesville.

Oh, what reason we have to be thankful that we as a company have escaped this scourge, with one exception—Brother Felt's [19] teamster had diarrhea for three days without applying for help and when he was helped it proved unavailing. A child of Brother Barney's,[20] 12 years old, hearing of this man's death took fright and was instantly seized with the cholera. This was at night; and during the night she was very bad and when I heard of it (tho poorly at the time) I felt so keenly that I went at once to render my assistance (if accepted) which was very cheerfully and though the symptoms were dangerous in that stage of the disease, I used the knowledge I gained on my trip from St. Louis to Kanesville and in due time brought about the favorable ones and she recovered rapidly.

The prolongation of our noon halt, (occasioned by the breaking of an axletree in the other ten of our division and we wait for them) has given me a chance to take some minutes of our journey up to this time. I have enjoyed myself well on the trip tho my health is poor and feel unequal to do my share of the work, but my mind is singularly easy on such things. I know that I acted to the best of my judgment in undertaking this journey and its consequent obligations. Knowing that my accommodations are as good as they possibly could be, I am content and often think of what Elder Taylor told me last winter in a blessing—*"That I should go up to Zion in peace."*

---

[19] This may have been Nathaniel Henry Felt who was in Edward Hunter's company. See Kate B. Carter, comp., *Heart Throbs of the West*, 12 vols. (Salt Lake City: Daughters of Utah Pioneers, 1939–51), 11:413.

[20] Royal Barney is listed as a member of Hunter's company in *ibid.,* 11:398.

August 11th—Since leaving Fort Kearney my health has been very poor—the very warm weather and the rain storms have prostrated my fragile constitution more than I could possibly expect, but having fortunately a Homepathic physician in our train (Doctor Smithy),[1] I take advantage of his [presence] having a little more faith in that practice than any other medical one.

We passed Ash Hollow [2] last Friday which presented quite a change of scenery, the bluffs having the appearance of decayed stone and the shrubbery presenting the greatest variety imaginable on wild soil. Several kinds of flowers as delicate and interesting looking as if they were raised in well cultivated gardens of the East. The buffalo are very numerous here. The scripture phrase—"The cattle upon thousand hills are the Lord's"—has a meaning in it. Before witnessing those animals it was ideal in a measure. My health did not permit me to relish their flesh but I heard others speak highly of its flavor.

[1] The homeopathic Dr. Smithy might well be the musician (Smithie) who helped to entertain at a party at the home of Howard Egan in Nauvoo (Juanita Brooks, ed., *On the Mormon Frontier: The Diary of Hosea Stout, 1844–1861,* 2 vols. [Salt Lake City: University of Utah Press and Utah State Historical Society, 1964], 1:55), and who was also listed by John D. Lee as one of the band that played at the dedication of the Nauvoo Temple.

[2] "The road usually taken west of Fort Kearny, along the south bank, went up the Platte and South Platte, then across the latter river and 19 miles north to reach the North Platte at Ash Hollow." See Dale L. Morgan, "The Reminiscences of James Holt: A Narrative of the Emmett Company," *Utah Historical Quarterly* 23 (1955): 166 n. 33.

Antelope is scarce but we killed one and its flesh I did relish. It was some like mutton. We have some choke cherries which make excellent pies.

August 15th—Just passed Court house rock and in sight of chimney rock and within one hundred miles of Laramie.[3] Our expedition in traveling had been materially felt, we often travel 17 miles a day and were it not for our occasional delays by loss of our cattle for a day or less than a day, the breaking of a wagon tongue or axeltree, our speed would be considerable. Our movements are as systematic as circumstances will allow Brother Wooley being a remarkably efficient man to keep a train straight and in order and he is blessed in having as material to work with in the shape of hands as could possibly be expected. Our practice is, except when the cattle are strayed or some accident, to start from seven to half past every morning, as Brother Wooley's policy is to Bait the cattle before starting and while they are doing so we women folks have plenty of time to prepare breakfast and cook for dinner. Our noon halt lasts about an hour and a half giving the cattle a chance to bait and water. The principle also is to stop one day in the seven as a Sabbath, but [not] arbitrarily on Sunday. Circumstances have to guide whether it be Saturday, Sunday or Monday.

August 17th—Saturday—Passed Scotts Bluffs [4] which presents a romantic appearance similar to the continuous chain that commenced at Ash Hollow. Indeed the scenery is much more interesting this side of that place than the other. Crossed Horse Creek at noon and we have halted in good season this evening in view of spending a pleasant Sabbath tomorrow, enjoying rest for ourselves but more especially for our cattle—that is, as is often remarked, our present salvation on this trip. A journey like this will teach a person to place a higher value on the animals appropriated to the service of man.

August 18th—Sunday—Instead of enjoying ourselves by having a good meeting as we proposed and expected that Brother Hunter's division would have met midway on the occasion, they have camped about one-half mile from us. But our airy castle was destroyed by a wet day. Preparing meals and washing dishes is not pleasant work in a rain storm outdoors. During the day Brother Campbell called

[3] Chimney Rock is a prominent landmark in northwestern Nebraska.

[4] Scotts Bluff, Nebraska, a well-known landmark on the Oregon and Mormon trails, was designated a National Monument in 1919.

to get some medicine for his wife who was dangerously ill from jumping out of the wagon when coming down a bad place in Ash Hollow and since has continued feverish and in great pain. She had **her infant in her arms.**

August 20th—Tuesday—This morning the cry of the cattle gone, to the amount of at least half, was anything but agreeable. Yesterday it rained nearly all day—making a two days' rain—which was the cause of the cattle straying. Towards noon part of them were found. We were divided off in parties going in all directions, distances of four to eight miles but before night they were all found—through the efficiency of Brother Segar who proposed at noon time that if a horse would be loaned him he would warrant the finding of the cattle. It so turned out—they were found about ten miles from the camp. Mrs. Campbell died yesterday[5] and their division lost cattle to about the same amount that ours did and in like manner found them.

August 21st—Wednesday—This morning [it] was supposable all difficulties had [been overcome] and were reckoned among the things that once were. It was e'en so in our division but in Brother Hunter's Brother Chase's horses were gone so that the ten he belonged to remained behind and we all started. This camping place supplied us abundantly with choke cherries, duly appreciated by all hands. Traveled nicely all day but oh the disaster of the evening. We had not been 15 minutes in carrel[6] when the cry—"The cattle are poisoned" saluted our ears. The slough water was rankly poisoned that it took immediate effect and in one hour's time one of the best oxen died and before retiring for the night two good cows. Others were effected some but recovered.

August 23—Friday—Within eight miles of "Fort Laramie" we make our halt at Mr. Bordeau's trading place (who formerly had his settlement at the fort but sold out to the States government).[7] His constant friendliness to the Mormons since the commencement of their journeying over these plains makes him interesting to us as people. I visited the Indian tents and was interested in observing their simplicity in living. They were principally occupied in drying

---

[5] Three Campbells died en route: Mary L., Benoni, and Lavina. See Carter, *Heart Throbs,* 11:404.

[6] The wagons were arranged in a ring for the night.

[7] James P. Bordeaux built a trading post eight miles downriver from Fort Laramie. The U. S. government had purchased the fort earlier. See Charles E. Hanson, Jr., "James Bordeaux," *Museum of the Fur Trade* 2 (Spring 1966): 2; and Edgar M. Ledyard, "American Posts," *Utah Historical Quarterly* 3 (1930): 95.

buffalo meat and tanning the skins, the squaws being the operators. One large tent caught my attention as having several squaws in it, one was elderly—probably mother to some of the others who were sitting around the tent with their little children round them. One was making patch work. The old squaw was packing away dried meat in a sack made of leather that looked some like vellum. It was painted fancifully and looked clean. We held some conversation by signs and called the other women's attention to my having no teeth, evidently a wonderment on their part.[8] The Indians have very handsome large teeth. I made signs to her about the children and their mothers. She pointed out the children of each mother. They were cleanly and handsomer than any I've seen before. The children were very handsome and smart looking. At another tent cooking was under operation and looked pretty good for a wild people. Another tent was characterized by its inmates—Indians and squaws looking quite stylish and gay, while gazing on them the Indian cried "Sue a Ochi", a few times before I realized its significance, meaning to depart. I afterwards learned they were, what is vulgarly termed, "sparking".

August 25th—Sunday—Yesterday camped within one mile of Fort Laramie on the river bank. Brother Hunter and Brother Woolley went there taking along the provision wagon to have it replenished which was accordingly done by a supply of flour, bacon and hams (flour $17.50 per hundred), also five yoke of cattle. Some of our best men had some thoughts of leaving here—an inducement of $60.00 a month for two months they thought had considerable attraction, together with vague reports that in the valley they could not earn more than their board. An hour's time consumed talking over the matter was all the difference caused. Next excitement, cattle missing. Tho nothing new, in the sound as disagreeable as the first time heard and while hunting them up Brother Smoot and his train came. This was the last chance of expectancy on Brother Haywood's part for his horse. It was seen and that was all.

Major Sanderson and two Aida camps [aides-de-camp] passed us which gave me an opportunity of seeing that personage (a fine looking man).[9] The mail passed us yesterday bringing general news from the valley that was good and Brother Haywood received a

---

[8] Not all of Martha's teeth were missing, as under her entry of September 23 she complains of a toothache.

[9] Maj. W. F. Sanderson commanded the garrison at Fort Laramie. Ledyard, "American Posts," p. 95.

18

letter from his lady that abundantly confirmed the general report. Also had the pleasure of perusing for the first time the 7th number of the first paper published in the Valley which was also confirmatory of good news.[10] Our cattle found and about starting going ahead of Brother Hunter's division. When about two hours on the road we were alarmed by most distressing cries of women and children. It was thought that the Indians were coming full speed upon us, by some, but soon found it was a wagon overturned caused by a stampede in Bishop Hunter's camp that were close behind us. I went up at once to render my services and amongst the wailing one female drew my attention. She seemed so beside herself and all she would say was, "I saw my Father killed and my mother is now dead; oh! What shall I do?" On realizing that the mother was not dead I went to see her and recognized Mrs. Condie.[11] She seemed insensible at first but in a little was conscious but very much frightened. She was laid on a bed, we supposing that she was much injured but to my great joy we found it not so. The only place I could find injured was between her shoulders and only slightly bruised. It seemed miraculous that she was not more. Her son-in-law did not escape so well. He had his leg broke which was rather trying as he (Merrill Rockwell) was considered a very efficient man in the camp. The stampede was caused by one of Bishop Hunter's horses running in among the cattle. I have heard that they are common among the cattle in that division but we have not had any as yet. They are very dangerous and are caused, I presumed, as much by mismanagement as accident.

I have seen the Rocky mountains for the first time today. They look stupendous in the dim opaque of the horizon and but a faint line marking their existence and altitude. The highest one is called "Laramie Peak". Our roads are excellent today—general health pretty good with the exception of Franklin Haywood [12] who has had a pull down causing a reaction of his old complaint (consumption) that has prostrated him for some days back. He is now on the gain and we have every hope that he will regain his health and a teamster being provided in his stead he will not be subjected to anxiety or be overworked—that and the heavy rains being the cause of his pull down.

[10] The *Deseret News* began publication on June 15, 1850. Issue no. 7, seen by Martha, was published on July 27, 1850, and contained news of the July 24 celebration, a request for volunteers to go to Little Salt Lake (Parowan), and items of interest to new arrivals.

[11] Several Condie women are listed as immigrants of 1850. See Carter, *Heart Throbs*, 11:407.

[12] A nephew of Joseph L. Heywood.

August 27th—Tuesday—Quite an excitement prevailed in our midst last night. About nine o'clock an animal was missing—not a quadruped but a biped answering the description of Bishop Haywood. After various remarks had been made on the occasion and sundry opinions advanced as to the suitableness of such unwarrantable freedom as to a biped losing himself, it was finally resolved by Capt. McPherson that if haply the stray was found he must be correlled and picketted for the night. This morning saw us on our way near three miles when he was discerned in company with another biped (Brother Smoot)[13] quietly awaiting us none the worse of wear but looking as happy as good company could make him.

August 29th—Thursday—The breaking of an axeltree has given me an opportunity to journalize a little and here I will record a providential incident. On Tuesday morning Sister Butterfield lost an ox and was obliged to start without making as much search as wished, which grieved her very sorely and did not feel reconciled to give up hunting him. In the course of the day an ox was found by Capt. Bary's ten (where she is) that was so weak from the "scours"[14] (evidently left behind by some forward company) that the men rejected him but Sister Butterfield thought she could cure him and drove him along with some trouble at first but today he travels well and turns out to be a better animal than the one she lost. Our axeltree is almost replaced and in ten minutes we will be rolling.

Yesterday we came along side our friend the Platte at the place where the brethren in coming from the Valley last fall encountered a large War party of Indians—about fifty miles west of Laramie. A communication was found from Brother Stratton indicating his coming from the Valley for the purpose of ascertaining the amount of emigration on the way and I believe aid them a little in knowledge of the latter part of the route; also an indication that Brother Woodruff's company were but five days [ahead]. We found notices from Brother Joseph Young's and Woodruff's[15] during the day and in the evening where we camped, sixty miles from

---

[13] Abraham O. Smoot had "engaged to bring out two trains of merchandise, one for Colonel John Reese [see Martha's entry of July 26], and conducted one for Livingston & Kinkade—the former by his partner, Jedediah M. Grant, the latter conducted by himself. These were the earliest of the merchant trains that supplied the Salt Lake City market after the one brought by Livingston & Kinkade the previous year." See Jenson, *LDS Biographical Encyclopedia*, 1:486.

[14] Diarrhea or dysentery.

[15] Both Wilford Woodruff and Joseph Young brought companies to Salt Lake Valley in 1850.

Laramie, we found another notice directed to the camp of Israel from Brother Stratton saying that Brother Woodruff's company had left them on the 25th, being but four days ahead of us.

August 30th—When passing Creek last evening and about corralling we found Brothers Stratton and Hanks from the Valley and Brother Whipple who left Bethlehem in Elder Woodruff's Company more than two weeks before we did.[16] They have had considerable sickness and twelve deaths on the journey and now detained by the greater number of their cattle straying away but they have found nearly all. We expect to corral along side of them tonight. Brother Stratton and Brother Hanks brought with them a letter from the President [Brigham Young] that was read to the camp last evening. It was good and interesting, detailing the prosperity of things in the Valley and backed by Brothers Stratton and Hanks. They will return after they see Brother Hunter's company and we expect Brother Haywood will accompany them. They think our train has done well but were expected by the President at an earlier date. The settled price of flour in the Valley at present is $25.00 per cwt. It was some of the time $1.00 per pound. It is expected it will fall some after the passing through of the California emigration.

They related a circumstances that spoke loud of the good state of things among the people in worldly matters. Last fall they set apart a piece of ground to cultivate for the use of the poor. They found two old ladies that was willing to be called poor but are not now willing as they earn about $3.00 a week and this was all the poor that could be found in the valley. There were other incidents related proving the prosperity of the place.

August 31st—Saturday—Last evening we corrlled along side Elder Woodruff's company and it was quite a pleasant meeting to those who were acquainted, but this was not my case but I had the pleasure of learning that Brother Lewens and family were well and had met with no accident by the way which gives me sincere pleasure. May the Lord bless him and his.

How much would I not give at times to see some choice spirits to mingle with as I was wont to do in past times and though "I go

---

[16] These men were probably Joseph A. Stratton; Ephraim Knowlton Hanks, pioneer of 1847, who went from the valley to meet Brigham Young's 1848 company on the Sweetwater, who was hired to take the mail across the plains in the winter of 1850–51, and who later assisted handcart companies into the valley; and Edson Whipple, who was a captain of fifty in Woodruff's company. See Jenson, *LDS Biographical Encyclopedia,* 2:765 and 3:561.

up to Zion in peace" how dreadful lonesome it is oftentimes. In the midst of spirits yet feeling all alone—yet what means more powerful to drive me to him who is greater than all earthly friends.

We had meeting at Elder Woodruff's camp last evening and he seemed to possess an excellent spirit from the remarks he made and deeply solicitous for the welfare of those under his care and manifested much pleasure in seeing our train come along. They had a great deal of sickness; one time all were sick. Twelve deaths—one was by lightening and three oxen with him, leaving a widow and children.

Today has been our Sabbath and the last day of the month. Our cattle had such a hard time yesterday that it was wisdom to rest them today. The roads are, at this part of the journey, very rough and hilly, little feed and water is scarce. We have had an uncommon fine day. Brother Woodruff's camp left about ten this forenoon and this evening part of Brother Hunter's division passed us and we learned his wagon broke down and delayed him back. Brothers Stratton and Hanks stay with us at present. We have had a very pleasant camping place and our buffalo meat relished well.

September 2nd—Monday—Had a fair day's traveling yesterday although part of the road was rough; journeying over the black is pretty hard on invalids and cattle but we are now past them once more on the bottom and keeping hard [by] the Platte. We overtook Brother Smoot's train and those of Brother Hunter's that were ahead. The air is and has been very invigorating for some days past. Frank gains but slowly. He has suffered from diarrhea for a few days. I think the fresh meat has been the cause of the change. Brother Haywood and the two brethren from the Valley have been absent from us for the two days, having gone back to Bishop Hunter's division.

September 5th—Friday—We have been travelling along the Willow Springs today over the mountains.[17] Our cattle begin to show the poverty and scarcity of water, the only pay they have for their hardest labor, roads being pretty rough and long days of travel. This morning we parted with our Valley friends, they taking with them Brother Haywood and he leaving his nephew very feeble, still suffering from diarrhea; I think rather worse today than any other, the jolting of the wagon I think is very injurious to him. His

[17] The company would appear to have been skirting the Laramie Mountains at their northernmost, following the North Platte or one of its tributaries.

uncle had him ride in the buggy for two days past—this was a relief to him so far and he missed the privilege today. Brother Richardson has taken upon himself to sleep with him and have a kindly care over him which is invaluable to Frank in his weakly state. And as far as my poor services shall go he shall have them as from an own sister. My health has been remarkable better today and that suddenly. All day yesterday I felt much prostrated and hardly power or wish to live and today I am not only well in body but happy in mind and feeling. I feel that there is a protecting power over me who can say to the stormy feelings within my breast "peace be still" as man cannot. How many proofs have I had of this during my pilgrimage but yesterday I was reasoned with and comforted by one who seeks to do me good, but all to little or [no] purpose and I lay down at night full of grief and dissatisfaction. This morning I arose calm, confiding and willing to do anything to confer happiness on my fellow creatures and all around me looked like friends. I felt in particular that it would be a great privilege to take care of Frank and be a comfort to him in the absence of his Uncle. Oh, may the God of Israel raise him up in health and strength in body and mind. Brother Woolley seems to miss his counsellor—very tender in his feelings regarding Frank's state and friendly towards me.

September 7th—Saturday—Camped this afternoon, half past one at Sweet Water [18] by side of the outskirts of the Rocky Mountain chain—335 miles this side of the Valley, within two miles of Saleratus Lake that we did not pass. Some of our men went to see it and brought some Saleratus from there.[19] We traveled ten miles today on sandy soil—rather hard for the cattle but very favorable to Frank who enjoyed the circumstance. This morning I was favorably impressed in regard to a change he boasted of when I first saw him. He felt that he was decidedly better, having perspired freely during the night and a few evacuations of water without diarrhea that had not occurred for sometimes previous. He sat in the chair during our travel, was lively and very communicative,

---

[18] The North Platte is joined by the Sweetwater southwest of present Casper, Wyoming, in Natrona County. The waters of the two rivers are presently impounded by Pathfinder Reservoir.

[19] Saleratus is potassium bicarbonate or sodium bicarbonate, commonly called baking soda. Harriet Page Wheeler Decker Young, a wife of Lorenzo Dow Young and one of three women in the pioneer company of 1847, baked some bread using saleratus, probably from this same lake. See Robert J. Dwyer, ed., "Diary of Lorenzo Dow Young," *Utah Historical Quarterly* 14 (1946): 162; William Clayton, *William Clayton's Journal* (Salt Lake City: Deseret News, 1921), p. 252.

often alluding to his feeling so much better. Perspiration continued. We were about six hours travelling and when camped instead of throwing himself on the bed, his usual custom he went out and sat with the men and ate a little biscuit crumbed in milk. In about an hour he returned to the wagon, lay down and acted quite drowsy during the rest of the day, his eyes half closed while sleeping. Had a passage about three o'clock and another tonight. Ate a little toast and chocolate for supper. The laudanum that was given during yesterday afternoon caused these symptoms, I should think, and I fear they are not very favorable. He took some more tonight. We came up to Woodruff's camp today but they went on while we stopped. Brother Haywood returned then the buggy and left his clothes which we received from them. No doubt he will have a hard time of it in riding all the way to the Valley.

September 8th—Sunday—Traveled twelve miles today. Passed right by Saleratus Lake and laid in a supply of the article and Independence rock.[20] All hands climbed its summit save myself and Frank but I could see that it was all covered with names and some of them I could read. After we corralled by the Sweet Water I took a tramp of 1½ miles to see the Devil's gate which we passed but could not see to advantage at that time.[21] It is a curiosity. Frank was very weak this morning—had two passages during the night but otherwise rested well. Acted more like himself this forenoon, sat up all the time we were riding in preference to laying down on account of the jolting. Had no passage until we carreled about five o'clock. He was very tired this evening but his symptoms decidedly better than yesterday.

As to myself I feel grateful to God for the peace of mind and health of body I enjoy. Everything wears a pleasant aspect around me, with the exception of Frank's health but I have hope for him and feeling a sympathy for him. I take pleasure in ministering to his wants. There is nothing unusual, or accident of any kind occured to us since Brother Haywood left us.

September 9th—Monday—Travelled 11 miles today, very pleasantly. We are camped by the Sweet Water, Rocky Mountains all around. Frank appeared decidedly better today. The traveling was over sand hills which favored him much. Walked about at noon time which he was not able to do yesterday. I visited Sarah Lawrence

[20] One of the most famous landmarks on the Overland Trail, the dome-shaped rock was covered with the names of travelers.

[21] The Sweetwater flows through this massive rock "gate."

at that time and though the conversation was carried on pleasantly, some knowledge imparted was calculated to make me feel sober and that the light heartedness and buoyancy of spirits I have been wont to feel will have to be given up for a variety of perplexities that are not known amongst the friends I have left.[22] How much I have thought today of the freedom that for years I have enjoyed to my hearts content; amidst all my vicissitudes I have enjoyed a freedom of thought and action that will never be known again. Oh that I may have strength according to my day. Excepting these reflectings the day passed very pleasantly and my health has been good. Rochester friends with all their endearments and their forebearances will pass before my mind and seeming to say, "Will you ever meet such again?" Well I enjoyed—I enjoyed them and their goodness in the day of it, and of my own will I left them to follow the fortunes of the Latterday faith and so far I have no serious cause to repent and I can say "Thus far the Lord has led me on".

[22] Sarah Lawrence, the discontented plural wife of Heber C. Kimball would seem to have brought up the subject of polygamy. While Martha no doubt knew about polygamy, the doctrine had not yet been publicly proclaimed by the church. Sarah's unhappiness probably gave Martha pause.

September 10th—Tuesday—We are camped at Bitter Cotton-wood Creek and 304 miles from the Valley. Traveled twelve miles over sand hills and crossed the Sweet Water twice. Last evening Doctor started on a hunting expedition but did not return. This morning when we were ready there was some uneasiness felt in our company. Brother concluded to turn out of corral on the road then start an expedition to hunt him up. We had not got on the road before he was descried. He had gone so far that in trying to return he could not descry our camp so had to wait till the sun arose this morning. He was unsuccessful but saw a panther.

Frank is gaining slowly but gradually and my hopes rise in proportion for him. I have so much confidence in this good moun-tain air as the best remedy for his disease. I wish I could realize its vivifying influence on myself today. I felt rather prostrated—I sewed pretty steady this forenoon mending shirts, etc. I felt unable to sit up this afternoon and under such an influence my thoughts are anything but agreeable. But like Corrinne, I make my own trouble, I act upon the impulse of my own warm nature and experience a delightful enjoyment in acting natural, even while prudence is con-tinually whispering in my ear that I am but treasuring up sorrow for this in the future. But yet like her I want to enjoy the present if it but yield a speck of enjoyment; well knowing " 'Tis all but a dream at the best". And I have had some moments of enjoyment on this trip (tho mingled with mortification) that perhaps will never return. Well let it be, I've had my streaks of sunshine during the pathway of life. What have I not enjoyed except a wedded life and its consequent happiness. And that is now the most dreaded thought. Liberty of conscience and action I have had for years and it has placed me where I am. In embracing Mormonism I followed the dictates of my own judgment, in opposition to that of my best and dearest friends, and may I be guided by the Spirit of God in what future steps I may take as I trust I was in that. And, oh! May I aim to do right in all the things notwithstanding my peculiar traits of character.

September 13—Friday noon—One week this morning since Brother Haywood left us. Frank gradually grows better. We have traveled eleven miles this forenoon. Day very cold. I have seen for the first time the snow capped Rocky Mountains. We are now about 270 miles from the Valley. Yesterday I had a delightful treat in having an opportunity of visiting some of my Kanesville friends— Sister Manning and Brother Hutchinson and family and Brother Pitt.[1] It was truly a commingling of spirits and has given me some animation that I have been destitute of for two or three days. There is to me such an oppressive spirit in my own company that I find it difficult to bear.

September 15th—Sunday—We have just met the expected teams from the Valley, first rate looking oxen. We traveled yesterday and on our carreling about sundown last evening were 250 miles from the Valley. Frank continues to gain daily. His spirits are good and also his appetite and [he] enjoys his food. I suffered yesterday afternoon with headache and very much at night. But this morning I feel well and in good spirits. The petty annoyances that are practiced towards me daily serve but to amuse me now. A plot yesterday formed against my peace turned rather bungling to the plotters. May the Lord bless those who are my friends and confound the plots of my enemies that they may get tired of such small business. The weather is very fine and truly healthy. Cold nights and mornings, clear sunshiny days. I suffer less now, or feel it less than I did some of our warmest days when I suffered so much from chills and cold sweat.

[1] Jacob F. Hutchinson and William Pitt were members of a band. Pitt, as band leader, was converted to Mormonism first, after which every member joined. They immigrated as a unit and sometimes gave concerts or appeared on special days. Pitt composed a special "Capstone March" for the dedication of the Nauvoo Temple. He died February 21, 1873, in Salt Lake City. See Brooks, *On the Mormon Frontier*, 1:55 n. 19.

September 17th—Tuesday—Yesterday we kept our Sabbath. Had good water and feed for the cattle. Today had good travel, crossed the South Pass bidding adieu to the Sweet Water and for the first time touching upon the Pacific Springs.[2] This day we have crossed the boundary of the Atlantic and Pacific sources. We have been coming up from the former and now we go down to the latter. It was keenly cold this morning but the sun shone clear and water [warmer?] during the day. I feel my health greatly improved. I can endure working without inconvenience and I would scarcely know it was so cold if I did not hear all around me complain. My spirits are good and my mind pretty clear, save one view of reflection. Frank continues to improve in health and was able to write a letter to his folks yesterday and does not seem to suffer from the exertion. We are now 225 miles from the Valley.

September 18th—Wednesday—Had a good days travel—very pleasing weather. Pretty late when we camped. Immediately Brother Woodruff rode up to us saying that he had been two nights and a day in the mountains, having met with some disasters concerning their horses and cattle—particulars I do not clearly understand.[3] Frank continues to gain but is not yet able to leave his wagon to walk but leaves it for an airing a few minutes before we start. This morning he milked two cows which tired him some. For the last three days we have seen Indians more or less passing along the road. Today I enjoyed a view of the Rocky Mountains on the western side, presenting to my mind a better appearance than the eastern side.

September 19th—Thursday—We travelled today over deep sand but made out about fifteen miles. We are now from the valley 179. This has been a warmer day than we have had for some time and I had a little of that oppressive feeling that I have suffered so much during the journey. Frank did not feel quite so well today and after sundown when we corraled, having overtaken Elder Woodruff's company, we have quite a large corral and had meeting on Brother Woodruff's side of the corral. Our trail on the road was very long,

[2] A miles wide pass through the Wind River Mountains in southwestern Wyoming, South Pass and its rediscovery by Jedediah Strong Smith contributed significantly to immigration in the 1840s and 1850s.

[3] Wilford Woodruff, apostle and fourth president of the LDS church, was involved in missionary work in the eastern United States when the First Presidency ordered him to "return to the Valley, and to bring with him all the Saints he could gather, and such means as could be collected from their properties and from contributions in the East." The Woodruff company arrived in Salt Lake City on October 14, 1850. See Matthias F. Cowley, *Wilford Woodruff: History of His Life and Labors* . . . (Salt Lake City: Deseret News, 1909), pp. 339–43.

having also Bishop Hunter's forward ten attached to our train and camped a mile from us.

September 22nd—Sunday—This evening we corralled at the fork of the Black River after a steady days travel. Last evening on our halting perceived a carriage and four horses. After leaving I found out that it was sent by Brigham Young for his sister, Mrs. Murray and Mrs. Persis Young.[4] I felt disappointed in not knowing that I could have seen Mrs. Murray and written by her until it was too late, but Sarah gave her all the particulars about Frank's health and brought him three potatoes and a piece of melon from her which was indeed a treat to him. He has been some troubled with his cough which he thinks proceeds from the bronchitis and causes him no alarm. He has taken a little cold but now being so near the termination of our journey I do not feel that uneasiness on his account that I did when Brother Haywood left. As to myself I feel a remarkable depression in reference to my arriving in the Valley. When I think of it a sober feeling comes over me that I cannot control. I never experienced this feeling that I know of, on going to any place previous. My health continues good—I do my work regular—sew considerably and read occasionally which is a relief to my general feelings. I have composed and written some verses to Mrs. Johnston and two pieces for the Guardian, besides some others for myself.[5] What an amusement this is for my lonely evenings after I do up my work— also our noon halt.

September 23—Monday—Traveled but a few miles this forenoon and halted for the day on a very pretty place by a branch of the _____ —140 miles from the Valley. I accomplished considerably of a washing this afternoon without any tax on my strength, nor felt the least tired when done which is very encouraging to me. I have suffered with a bad tooth ache steady all day, but this is a trifle to me after suffering as I have in prostration of strength the most part of this trip. This morning I got a blessing from our captain—of his particular kind but it hurt me not. Frank's health is more consequence to me than the pleasing of our captain and his lady. He does not feel quite so well tonight. I think he sat in the

---

[4] Fanny Young Murray was an older sister of Brigham Young. See James Amasa Little, "Biography of Lorenzo Dow Young," *Utah Historical Quarterly* 14 (1946): 69 n. 22. Persis Goodall Young was a wife of Lorenzo Dow Young and hence Fanny's and Brigham's sister-in-law. Ibid., p. 171.

[5] "Mrs. Johnston" was probably the mother of Joseph E. Johnson with whom Martha lived for a short time in Kanesville. The poetry was destined for the *Frontier Guardian* at Kanesville.

wind too much this afternoon and ate a piece of pie. His diarrhea returned while his cough seems gaining ground.

About six o'clock this evening Brother Woolley's son and a young man with a wagon and seven yoke of oxen from the Valley came, bringing with them vegetables and potatoes. I had a note by them from Brother Lewens who had a prosperous time during his journey. About an hour after they arrived two brethren from the Valley rode up to camp with us for the night on their way to Bishop Hunter's company to hurry them on. I heard that Brother Haywood arrived in the Valley, Sunday the 15th and Brother Woolley's son started next day without hardly seeing him. I also heard Brother Hyde does not start till the first of the month. Good news all the time from the Valley.

September 24th—Tuesday—Had a good days travel of 17 miles but most unpleasant on account of a strong head wind and the dust flying thicker than ever before. We have carreled along side of Black Fork. Frank suffered some from hard travel and dust but is better than yesterday. The partial return of his diarrhea seemed to ease his cough. My toothache continued bad till I fell asleep late last night and this morning my face was swollen very much—made me feel quite sickish and prostrated all day. This afternoon I could not sit up but this evening I feel better tho my face aches some.

September 25—Wednesday—We are now at Fort Bridger, 113½ miles from the Valley.[6] Had a good days travel through rough, very pleasant day and very good camping place. Boys are enjoying themselves with music and dancing. Frank's health some better today. Had a good night's rest last night. I did not suffer today with face ache but my spirits were rather depressed. I committed myself this morning (for the first time since Brother Haywood left) by giving way to an ebullition of feeling bordering on resentment. And getting up rather later than usual having so much to do about Frank's wagon I was excited in my feelings to get everything in order, our teamster behaved uncivil to me and I allowed my temper to get the upper hand of me. Elder Rin has been anything but obliging to me since Brother Haywood left us, nor does he as much [as] milk a cow for some time, not withstanding Brother Woolley scolds

[6] Fort Bridger, established by James Bridger and his partner Louis Vasquez, was the last supply station before reaching Salt Lake Valley. So vital was it to the Mormon immigration that the LDS church purchased it in 1855. For details of this controversial transaction see Fred R. Gowans and Eugene E. Campbell, *Fort Bridger: Island in the Wilderness* (Provo: Brigham Young University Press, 1975).

so much about. For the first time I remembered how many little things Brother Haywood would do for me about starting time, particularly when I was in a hurry. We have heard this evening from the Valley through a person in this place, that Elder Hyde will not leave till the 15th of the next month.

September 26th—Thursday—Had a good days travel and we camped at Muddy Creek. This evening the two brethren returned from Brother Hunter's camp. They are about two days behind us— some families short of provisions. Frank is about the same—the riding was hard for him today. This morning I received a greater blessing than previous arising from a simple remark I made to Mrs. Ballard was told, "I might go to Hell for all he cared, was not worth the rope that would hang me" applied an epithet to me that I did not hear prefaced by the word Irish, that he had never been insulted so much by anyone before as he had by me for the last 600 miles of the journey and that I need not think I can rule everything "though I be from Ireland".

Since Brother Haywood left us there seems to be a particular satisfaction to utter forth his insulting remarks so loud that the whole camp can hear all he says, what his object is in so doing I cannot conceive for I am very careful in my conduct, remaining in the wagon all the time we travel and attending faithfully to my work when we camp. Occasionally some errand calls me to Mrs. Butterfield but it is solely on Frank's account and this gives great offense, but I cannot submit to such an infringement of liberty or the slightest inconvenience to my patient, he was left in my charge as also in Mrs. Butterfield's and I cannot feel that I have erred in any respect since Brother Haywood left us.

October 1st—Tuesday—This evening we are camped 39 miles from the Valley. Today and yesterday had hard travelling, crossing the creek so often and going up and down hills in crossing the mountains. The scenery has been very grand for the last few days, the rocks are so magnificent looking and the mountains so high and perpendicular that it delights, especially being interspersed with shrubbery and small wood in their coats of rich autumnal grandeur. How much it would enhance the pleasure of the contemplation if I had wherewith to say to "How delightful"—but no!, pent up in a wagon, only one place to look out and the most uncompaniable sitting right before all day watching my every movement to find fault with both action and word— whose remarks have nothing of any interest in them to me, being mostly about eating and cooking—

31

a theme that I always despised. But Frank is sick and I try to bear with it as patiently as I can but still it's hard. And the teamster's incivility deprives me of getting out of the wagon as I was wont to do when Brother Haywood was with us. A report came from the Valley by a brother and another son of Brother Woolley's that he had taken him a wife since his arrival there, in which I put no credence. This morning the brother and the sons of Woolley's left us to meet us on our arrival to the Valley with Flag, etc.[7] Brother Woolley wants to have a great display of his train of which I have no desire to form a part. Frank has coughed distressingly last night and today. I notice when his diarrhea ceases his cough is hard. He is much disappointed in his uncle not sending for him, or even sending him a line or message of any kind. He remarked today that it was his new wife that prevented him.[8]

October 2nd—Wednesday—A rainy morning greeted us to commence the duties of the day and when we got fairly started Smoot's train was in the road to our inconvenience. About ten o'clock my thoughts were taken off of everything connected with our train by the appearance of Brothers J. E. Johnston and Hyde, making their appearance on their return. I spent about half an hour with Brother Johnston who entertained me with a relation of his own affairs, which were prosperous and also the arrangement he made for my reception amongst his relations, which makes my prospects on entering the Valley rather different from what they have been—how kind, how free hearted, how confiding in his friendship, how congenial his spirit. He is a noble soul and I feel warmly interested in his welfare and why not? I feel to owe him a debt of gratitude for his kindness to me when a stranger. Our traveling has been very hard today and towards night the wagon Mrs. Ballard rides in was upset while she was in it and most fortunately escaped; with the exception of a lame wrist and the spoiling of her bonnet and caps there was little damage done. None of the company's goods were injured.

While the wagon was getting to rights Brother Haywood came to us to take Frank away. How different I felt to meet him to what I did to see Brother Johnston. My feelings are so chilled when I think of going to Brother Haywood's house.

[7] The arrival of an immigrant company in the valley was often occasion for a ceremonial welcome.

[8] This would be Sarah Symonds, Heywood's second wife.

A GOOD MAN BUT NOT INTERESTING 4

Salt Lake Valley—October 13th—Sunday—Last Sabbath arrived here to Bishop Haywood's [1] house and I can say according to Elder Taylor's prediction that "I have come up to Zion in peace" for any trouble I had was made by another without provocation, and hurt me not! My health has been but poorly since I arrived but feel much better. The evening of my arrival I had an interview with Sister Kimball (with whom I was made acquainted by Mrs. Hale in Rochester) [2] and was much pleased with her and the warm reception I received, and in two days after a similar one from Elder Kimball. I spent Friday to their home and was well entertained but especially in the evening in hearing Elder Kimball's fireside conversation. Have had an opportunity this week of getting acquainted with Mrs. Franey Kimball [3] who has been assisting Mrs. Haywood in sewing. She is mighty in doctrine and being Scotch she has their force and determination of character, very conspicuous. She is not so pleasing to me as other females. Mrs. Haywood is much reserved in her manner towards me but I admire her very much. She is the

[1] Heywood's home was located on the south side of present 200 North between Main Street and West Temple.

[2] Several of Heber C. Kimball's wives came from New York.

[3] Probably Frances Swan Kimball, a native of Scotland and a wife of Heber C., who came to Utah in 1848. Later she moved to California where she married a non-Mormon named Clark. See Kate B. Carter, ed., *Our Pioneer Heritage,* 17 vols. (Salt Lake City: Daughters of Utah Pioneers, 1958–), 10:408–9.

personification of a good wife and in such matters I feel very small beside her.

Last evening I received baptism at Brother Haywood's hands and this morning was confirmed by him and Brother G. A. Smith and expected to receive my patriarchial blessing from Father John Smith, his father, but his health was not very good and so deferred it but was made happy in my acquaintance with them as Mother Johnston belonged to him and Joseph E. spoke of me to the family, in a particular manner.[4] Attended meeting and heard a discourse from Amasa Lyman on the Gold excitement that was interesting though nothing new to the operating of my mind.[5]

October 27th—Sunday—The weather has been delightful during the last two weeks and my health has improved daily so that I now feel in better health than at anytime in Pottawatomie and consequently my enjoyment increases but I do not feel as wont to do among my dear friends in Rochester but the prospect is fair that I will in time. Mrs. Haywood continues in my favorable estimation and as her reserve towards me begins to wear off her society is pleasanter as also with Mrs. Vary.[6] Last Sunday morning I received my patriarchial blessing from Father Smith. One trait of my character referred to pleased me much, "That I should have wisdom to act in the best possible way in all circumstances that I may be placed in". It is a confirmation of my own thoughts on this point as regards to the past while some have supposed I acted unwisely on such an occasion or another. I felt assured that I had taken the course under the circumstances because guided by the spirit within. And now at this time may the Lord grant me wisdom to think aright and power to conduct myself according, is the sincere desire of my heart. I realize that instead of having a friend to consel with or ask advice of, I have to depend as it is solely on myself and if it will be the means

---

[4] Joseph E. Johnson's parents, Ezekiel and Julia, were separated. On the advice of Joseph Smith, Jr., Julia was sealed to John Smith ca. 1843 at Nauvoo. John Smith was Joseph Smith's uncle and the father of George A. John served as the third presiding patriarch of the LDS church. See Johnson, *Trail to Sundown,* pp. 74, 80.

[5] Amasa M. Lyman, one of the Twelve Apostles, had returned from a mission to California on September 30, 1850. The following year Lyman and Charles C. Rich were to head a company of Mormons to San Bernardino. See Albert R. Lyman, *Amasa Mason Lyman, Trailblazer and Pioneer* (Delta, Ut.: Melvin A. Lyman, 1957), pp. 204–5.

[6] Sarah Symonds, according to Heywood family folklore, was called "Mrs. Vary" because she was like the girl who "was very, very good, and when she was bad, she was horrid." The children called her "Nana," and later Martha came to call her the more familiar "Sister Vary."

of throwing [me] more immediately to depend on the Lord, in all, my present loneliness will terminate in a blessing.

I made a call on Sister Eliza Snow and was so pleased with her that I was persuaded to remain the afternoon. Found Sister Murray there. Saw and had an introduction to Brigham Young.[7]

This morning felt rather careless about going to meeting but after hearing George A. Smith and Brigham Young I felt that I would have been a loser. I felt in hearing Brigham's remarks that it affected my mind and feelings. The teachings of both were comprised in George A.'s text—Obedience is better than Sacrifice, etc. and what was said I could give a hearty Amen to. I am now three weeks here and though I find a perceptible difference in the manners of the people to what I have been used to, and no doubt I appear to disadvantage to them, yet I think after a while I will enjoy myself better. If once started in the path of usefulness I know I shall be happy. It used to be a common remark with me when actively engaged in religious pursuits, "That out of the path of duty there was no real happiness".

I have been down to Benjamin Johnston's once the last week.[8] He expressed a little surprise at my not going there to visit, but there is something for-bidding in the appearance of the place to me. Sister Snow remarked to me that I might consider myself fortunate in getting a home to Bishop's Haywood. I may yet feel the force of her remarks when I get better acquainted in this place. The Mail started from here last Monday and I sent a letter to Mrs. Strong, Mrs. Hall, Mr. Murray and Joseph E. Johnston.

November 3rd—Sunday—Snowstorm set in Friday, the first of the month, and today it is being washed away by rain which makes the day very dull and miserable, and of course, no meeting held.

November 10th—Monday [November 11]—5 o'clock—Rose this morning at an unusually early hour. Brother and Sister Haywood supposing that Frank was in the act of dying, for the last 24 hours he has had the appearance of any moment departing and

[7] Eliza R. Snow, sister of the fifth LDS president, Lorenzo Snow, had been sealed to Joseph Smith, Jr., on June 29, 1842. She came to Utah in 1847 and was married to Brigham Young in 1849. Sister Murray was Brigham's sister.

[8] Benjamin Franklin Johnson was a brother of Joseph E. The earliest plat of Salt Lake City shows Benjamin's lot on the northwest corner of present 400 West and South Temple streets. Martha would have had to go "down" to his place since the Heywood property was on lower Capitol Hill.

will probably within another 24 hours. He now lays in his usual quiet state and in this he has been remarkably favored, caused principally by the usual expectoration in consumption producing the distressing cough, passing off by diarrhea, sparing him much pain and those around him. Doctor Sprague has been the physician— the others have been consulted but without effect.[9]

I was favored yesterday with a call from Brother William Snow and his wife (who was Sister Winds) that I esteem so highly and enjoyed a few moments happiness in their society.[10] Last week I made a call on Brother Joseph and Mrs. Young, which afforded me a similar enjoyment. And thus it is with me, that these transient flashes of enjoyment are ever the means of giving pleasure and breaking up the monotonous opaque of dull every day business, but more especially if I am located where I cannot indulge in the natural current of my buoyant spirits. How much Mr. Haywood reminds me of my brother whose pecularities I never could endure. But Mr. Haywood is less of the critique and also less interesting because not so intellectual as my brother—but he is a good man but not interesting. Mrs. Haywood is a "nopassed" in housekeeping for a young woman with too much care to do justice to her natural abilities in other spheres and youth. It pains me to see a woman in the prime of her youth tied down to the responsibility of a large family.[11]

November 17th—Sunday—Last Tuesday Frank's spirit left this state of existence for another clime. He clung to life to the last. About three hours before death he stood up on the floor for a few minutes

[9] Dr. Samuel Linzey Sprague came to Utah in 1848, one of the first doctors to arrive in Salt Lake City. He planted the first flower garden from bulbs and seeds he brought from Boston. See Frank Ellwood Esshom, *Pioneers and Prominent Men of Utah* (Salt Lake City, 1913), p. 1179. In her book, *The Mormon Prophet and His Harem* (Cambridge, Mass., 1866), Mrs. C. V. Waite tells how Dr. Sprague had just moved into his new house in 1862 when Brigham Young came and coolly told him that he would like it for his wife Emeline for three or four years until he could build her another. The Spragues could live in the house formerly owned by Jedediah M. Grant which would be repaired and cleaned for their use. "Emeline, who is really a kind-hearted creature, came and wept with Sister S., saying she did not want the home, 'but Brigham has set his mind upon it, and we don't any of us *Dare* to speak to him about it.' " (pp. 264–65.)

[10] William Snow came to Utah in 1850 with Wilford Woodruff's company (Carter, *Heart Throbs*, 11:445). His wives as of 1850 were Hannah Miles, Lydia Adams, Sallie Adams, and Jane Maria Shearer to whom he had been married less than a month at the time of the visit to Martha. See Jenson, *LDS Biographical Encyclopedia*, 3:520.

[11] The Heywood home had in it besides the two wives, Sarepta and Sarah (Mrs. Vary), the invalid Frank Heywood, Martha, and Sarepta's daughter, Alice, and brother, Theodore Blodgett.

after having one of his spells which was not quite so severe as his former ones. He remarked himself that he tried to overcome its influence. About nine o'clock at night he showed symptoms of another spell and at once apprehended it would be his death struggle. After struggling for half an hour, conscious all the time, his pulse ceased to beat, his hands relaxed but his breath did not leave him for an hour. Had no power to speak or notice anything. He died very quietly at half past ten o'clock. His funeral took place on Wednesday at 3 o'clock, Brother Kimball making some excellent remarks on the nature of departed spirits and their existence. Wished "that our friend Frank had been baptized even without his faith, that then he would be in the fold and the Shepherd would look after him. O but yet he was in a better state having acted up to the best light he had he was much better off than many who have embraced this work and do not act up to the light they have". He also touched upon the subject of a great calamity coming on this people if they continued in their present state of indifference. During his speaking I felt that I for one would try and do my duty as far as it was made known to me. May the Lord grant me strength to do right in all things. We followed him to the burial ground which surprised me much by its multiplicity of occupants, a great number being California emigrants.

Today attended meeting and heard a funeral sermon from G. A. Smith on the death of a brother Perkins who died one year ago and Sister Perkins, a Sister-in-law who died one week ago. From meeting I went to see Brother and Sister Lewens [12] and was pleased to find them in comparatively pleasant circumstances, being in a house and having plenty to eat and best of all good health. Brother Hale accompanied me and we had a very pleasant visit indeed.

November 24th—Sunday—Today we occupied the addition of the house for the first time [13] and was seemingly enjoyed by all the family—especially this evening in having a Bishop's meeting and being wet weather it would have been otherwise unpleasant. The President, Brethren P. P. Pratt, Woodruff, G. A. Smith met with them.

Attended meeting and heard the President speak on the principle of receiving the truth in the love of it, his remarks were truly delight-

---

[12] Lewens was the man who had baptized Martha in Canada. She retained a great affection for this couple.

[13] The Heywoods had added a large living room on the front of their home. That, together with a porch, would make living conditions better for all.

ful to me and I know that I have always loved the principles he advanced and taught the people. G. A. made a few remarks in reference to the mission of Iron County, or little Salt Lake. After meeting I called to Elder Kimball's and had the privilege of an hours private conversation with him, the result of which bringeth peace to my mind. Elder Kimball has been ill for the last week of the quincy but is better now. I know that my mind is clearer and better than heretofore and hope it will continue to grow clearer. My prospect of work increases every day, so much so that I feel a difficulty in accomplishing what is before me at this present time.[14] The mail went out this last week and I mailed a letter to my Brother in Canada and was disappointed in not sending one to Brother Johnston whose affairs in this place be any but a gloomy aspect. This last week had the news of a territorial government being given to us and the different officers nominated.

December 1st—Sunday—Last week some little incidents occurred. Wednesday called for the first time to Brigham Young's and appointed to go there tomorrow to make his cap. My cap trade increases very fast. Called to Brother Woolley's store and received the flowers he promised me on the way.[15] Also called to William Snow's. His first wife [16] is not long for this world, I fear. Friday evening attended a ball at Bishop Hendrick's [17] in company with Brother and Sister Haywood. Enjoyed myself very well. In consequence of it raining hard we did not get home till five o'clock next morning. Was not acquainted with any lady there. Met Brother Hutchinson which afforded much pleasure.[18] Had some singing during the evening. A Brother Ferguson recited an Irish piece with true native eloquence which interested me very much.[19] Supper was

[14] Martha made caps and hats for men, taking individual orders. Later, as she was able to get materials and trimmings, she would make women's hats. Hatmaking and teaching school were her means of support for many years.

[15] Edwin Woolley and Joseph L. Heywood were partners in a business enterprise, according to this notice that appeared in the *Deseret News* on January 11, 1851: "Messrs. Heywood & Woolley have removed their goods to the north room of the New Store House."

[16] Hannah Miles.

[17] Probably James Hendricks, first bishop of the Nineteenth Ward. He was crippled for life at the "battle of Crooked river" October 25, 1838, while helping defend the Saints against a mob in Missouri. He came to Utah in 1848. See Jenson, *LDS Biographical Encyclopedia*, 2:403.

[18] This may have been Jacob Flynn Hutchinson, a member of Hunter's 1850 pioneer company and a member of the 1850 legislature. See Esshom, *Pioneers and Prominent Men*, p. 233.

[19] Possibly James Ferguson who had been a sergeant-major of Company A, Mormon Battalion, and later adjutant-general of the Utah militia and territorial attorney. Ibid., p. 114.

served at an early hour to which I did ample justice. Its style and variety was admirable for this place. Spent yesterday in preparing Mrs. Vary's wagon for my sleeping apartment, she having taken up her abode in the new addition of the house. I anticipate some comfort in it with the exception of stormy weather—its dampness then is very disagreeable.

My mind has been somewhat more calm this last week on the all absorbing subject that has engrossed it for the last five months, yet it is far from being tranquil or happy but I have not allowed my thoughts to wander in other directions since my conversation with Brother Kimball. Yet, to some extent they do and probably will till I cease to be my own. I sent a letter to Joseph E. this last week and put in the slip of paper we agreed upon. Mr. Hall spent the greater part of yesterday here and helped me to move my things and fix my wagon for me. It made the day very pleasant to me. There is an exhibition under way and I have had an invitation to take part but will not for two reasons—first, I believe that Brother Haywood would not be willing to have me and secondly it is composed of young men apart from any responsibility of the brethren of the church, not one of the Kanesville association being with them.

I did not attend meeting today on account of the weather and not feeling very smart from the effects of being up all Friday night and hard work yesterday, spent the most of the day regulating my things. I have enjoyed Mrs. Haywood's society more the last week than previously and think I will the longer I am acquainted, if certain arrangements do not interfere with her apparent good feelings manifested towards me.

December 8th—Sunday—We have had remarkably cold weather during the last week commencing with a snow storm last Sunday night, succeeded by a very severe frost. I spent Monday pretty much finishing up my wagon arrangement. Tuesday went to Brigham Young's and worked on his fur cap till dark but would have remained but for engaging to make a cap for G. A. Smith as a present for his Iron Co. expedition.[20] Wednesday worked on it and sent it in the evening and had the satisfaction to know that it suited him well. Next morning went to Brigham's and finished his cap and though he was sick abed Mrs. Young ascertained that he was

---

[20] George A. Smith led the expedition to settle Little Salt Lake (Parowan) in the winter of 1850–51. See Gustive O. Larson, ed., "Journal of the Iron County Mission, John D. Lee, Clerk," *Utah Historical Quarterly* 20 (1952), for a full account.

pleased with it. I also made her a cap and neck-fixing. The Youth's Theatrical Society met here three times last week and have elected Brother Campbell for their president. I have been called upon to take a part but have not yet decided to do so. I wish to see the Society in existence on strictly moral principles and for intellectual improvement and did I give my services to it, it would be purely to give an impetus to the carrying out of these principles. The combination of the human mind is always the better in uniting the sexes. It makes men more moral and polite in their deportment and expands the minds of females and gives them a more intellectual turn and I consider it a higher order of amusement than Balls or the common run of entertainment. There are conversational entertainments that I delight in but like angels visits, few and far between. During the last week the Legislature has been in session.[21]

Yesterday we had the little stove set up in the large room, after waiting such a length of time for the elbow. It heats the room very thorough and burns but little wood. In the afternoon we had the company of Mrs. Crosbis and Miss Savage. The latter I have quite a liking for and her journey to this place being round by the Pacific Coast and sojourn in San Francisco, makes her company interesting. In the evening Mr. Barlow with whom I made some acquaintance to Benjamin Johnston's called with a young man of the name of Cunningham who came out this last year from Ireland. He favored us in singing two Irish songs in the rich peculiar style of his native home. Mr. Barlow is a Kentuckian and appears to be a very fine man.[22]

For the last two days I have had the blues. I think I took a little cold in returning from Brigham's Thursday evening. It was so intensely cold. Mr. Haywood is also complaining.

December 15th—Sunday—Disagreeable day outdoors, snowing and raining. Last week very mild pleasant weather. Mr. Haywood is poor in health all the week and continues so today; has not been able to attend to his business of late. I have been depressed in spirits and tho I appreciate and feel grateful for a good temporary home there is a spirit pervading that seems to weight down my spirits, nor can I rise above it, tho I often try. But from a conversation with Mrs. Haywood yesterday I shall think of changing my

[21] This entry illustrates so well Martha's work for a living and her joy in cultural activities.

[22] This may have been James M. Barlow, a Kentuckian who came to Utah in 1850. See Carter, *Heart Throbs*, 11:398.

home as she thinks we will be mutually benefitted by it.[23] I pray God to direct me in thoughts and steps and may I do nothing that I shall have to repent of, or be permitted to associate with any evil company. Sarah Strange has been working for us for the last week at dressmaking.

Since writing the foregoing have had an interview with Brother Haywood, counselling me as usual to assist Mrs. Haywood which I am well aware would be good for my health.

December 22nd—Sunday—Dry cold weather during the last week. I took a more active part in house matters and I believe in so doing have had better health. I feel much better today than last Sunday and the improvement has been gradual. Turned off ten caps during the week.[24] Did not leave the house till Friday forenoon when I obeyed a summons from Mrs. Butterfield who is very sick and wanted to see me. I spent the day with her and was surprised to find her so low. Went there today in company with Mrs. Kimball and her daughter and found her no better. I think her life very precarious. Sarah has her duties much increased by this calamity.

Called over last evening to Elder Kimball's who suffers from a cold but the family generally well.

Our Elocution speculation has progressed so far as to assume the prospect of an exhibition advertised to take place next Thursday evening and we are all on tiptoe excitement as to the result.

Rumours have been afloat during the last week the Indians have robbed and destroyed the lives of the last company of California emigrants on their way to the mines. It is said that Walker and his tribe has done the deed and his brother is the one to tell the tale who professed to abhor the act. If this is so t'will probably be the commencing of hostilities in this place. I have a foreboding that there is something besides prosperity for us as a people in this place and often has the remark been made—the Lord has us in a place where he can do with us as he lists.

My mind seems to have lost its peculiar enjoyment that it used to possess without an abiding pleasure. I feel in a measure to have lost the charm of existence for a season but I hope it is but for a

---

[23] Sarepta was only human in her feeling toward Martha—that she might find another place to live to their mutual advantage. Heywood apparently did not realize that this capmaker, hatmaker, schoolteacher had had no experience in cooking and other household chores, a lack that must have been keenly felt by both women since Sarepta was such a meticulous housewife.

[24] To turn out ten caps in a week should have enabled Martha to contribute toward household expenses. Her taking "a more active part in house matters" should have helped to alleviate tensions.

season as I know that if this work is of God I have an important part to act if he spares my life. But for the present I breathe in an atmosphere of uncertainty as it were.

December 29th—Sunday—Last Sabbath of the year of 1850. The weather remarkably fine tho very cold during the nights and mornings but in the day the sun shines very warm indeed. Regret that I did not attend meeting today as Brigham Young preached. Brother Haywood was the only one of the family that went. He is some better as he was to business some of the week and also to a party Christmas eve a few miles out of town to Brother Winallis. I had an invitation but did not go on account of the rehearsals. Our Exhibition came off Friday evening with much credit to our society.[25] We had a full house and our receipts were $100.32 and allowed us a dividend of $2.70 to each. Brother Brigham has told the Society to go on with our performances. This last week has passed much more agreeably to me than the former ones since my arrival in this place. The mingling in society is so congenial to my feelings that the absence of it is calculated to give me low spirits in ruminating on my own circumstances. Sister Butterfield is some better. Sarah acted her part better than I expected she would and also Sister Frances Kimball but Miss Badlam has a decided theatrical talent and as far as my judgment goes I hail her as a future star of the stage. Mr. Barlow in Maw Worm did well but was objected to by some on account of not ommitting some plain speeches in his sermon. This people being rather fastidious on account of their ignorance.

This time last year I was in Kanesville in the midst of its festivities.

New Years Day—Monday evening our Elocution Society met and adopted a constitution as a basis for our association, previously approved of by the President (Brigham Young) and they also decided on producing Hamlet for the near Exhibition. Mr. Barlow excused himself from taking part in the exercises on the plea of not having time to spare but desires to be considered an honorary member. Attended a Ball on this evening to Pack's house which I enjoyed much as the company were very select and a very free

---

[25] Of the exhibition on Friday night, December 27, 1850, Hosea Stout wrote: ". . . In the eve attended an Exhibition at the Bowry. There was a variety of Dramaticks, Farces, Songs, dances, music &c after which a grand display of fireworks of sky Rockets &c. all together it was a tolerably good time." Brooks, *On the Mormon Frontier*, 2:386.

spirit pervaded. Brother Haywood was expressly invited to preside as Bishop and accordingly opened the Ball with prayer. Our picnic supper was very good. While at the Ball Mr. Barlow called to see me and invite me for William's Ball Friday evening. He spent the evening with Sister Vary. The news of Brother Haywood's expected Southern Tour became public this evening.

Yesterday called to see Sister Butterfield who is still very low. Today I had a conversation with Brother Haywood who hinted at the probability of wanting me to go with him South which is a new train of thought to me of a very agreeable nature.[26] This field of labor is one that I would delight to act in—that of a missionary and a wife. The former I believe I have a natural talent for and privation would be nothing in the discharge of it.

[26] Heywood had only "hinted" at the possibility of taking Martha with him, but it set her hopes soaring.

January 5th, 1851—Sunday—[1] Last year at this time I was in Kanesville (1850) living to Brother Joseph E. Johnston's, enjoying the prospect of coming to this place, having at that time heard such a glowing description of it from the brethren who came down there from this place. The year before I was in Rochester (1849) and I call to mind some circumstances of interest. I was not then a Mormon nor had I made up my mind to become one, but just at that time Mr. Hall returned from Philadelphia where he was baptized in the Church and ordained an Elder. He was delayed a week in Rochester on his return to Canada and gave me his company every evening conversing on the subject of Mormonism. A short time previous I received a letter from Mr. White [after] an omission of his correspondence for nearly two years and also a letter from Mr. Lewens. I was then surrounded by Advent friends and also some of my Baptist ones, especially Mrs. Strong and her connections. (1847) The year before I was boarding to Mrs. Gibson (my friend) and was suffering very much with the disease of my eye, obliged to keep it bandaged up continually. (1846) The year before was to Mr. Hayes on his farm at which time I was in very low spirits on account of my

---

[1] This entire entry is a good resumé of Martha's life going in reverse. By careful reading one may piece together her activities. Aside from her religious activities, she seems to have had a rather trying relationship with an unknown "Mr. P."

health which was very poor at the time and the summer previous. The year before I was in the wilds of Canada West as an Advent preacher engaging in the prospect of the coming of the Saviour enduring the scoffs and privations that attend such a course. Then I had not heard the first lisp of Mormonism and thought there was nothing ahead of the Saviour's coming.

The year before I was in the city of New York living with my father and stepmother and my sister Ellen lived near to us. Was very strong in the Advent faith to the annoyance of my relatives. My sister Anna Maria died the November previous, who lived in Brooklyn leaving her husband and four children to mourn her loss and those I occasionally saw; shortly before her death my brother Andrew was in New York and had the pleasure of seeing him twice, once to my sister Ellen's and again in the street at which time he passed—so great was his repugnance to me on account of my being a religionist and I have never seen him since. I was then making caps to Mr. George Alvord's establishment, one whom I had a very pleasant acquaintance with. I left New York in June following and not been there since. My father died the following winter and since the knowledge of that event I have never heard from those relations.

The year before this I was enjoying a very interesting visit to Elder Sawyer's family in Keesville (1843) with whom I made acquaintance when living in Schenectady.

The year before was in Rochester in Mr. Hayes (1842) ——— enjoying religion very much as a comfort for a severe trial I endured in respect to my acquaintance with Mr. P.———

The year before was also in Rochester (1841) in Mr. Hayes enjoying religion and also the society of Mr. P. Made a trip to Canada for the first time the first week in February and spent three months there visiting my father and my Brother's family. The year previous was in Schenectady.

January 12, 1851—Sunday—Last Monday Mrs. Vary went a-visiting and previous to her leaving in the morning I perceived that Mrs. Haywood had some intelligence to make her more than usually excited. And as I had reason to know the cause I took the opportunity of Mrs. Vary's absence to open a conversation that I had but waited a favorable opportunity of Mrs. Vary's absence of doing so. The cause of her uncontrolable grief on this morning was Mr. Haywood's communicating to her the probability of taking me south, which she could not bear in addition to her other troubles and this made the rest appear but light. She expressed her feelings that in the event

45

of my coming into the family she thought it but reasonable that I should remain with her to be a help in Brother Haywood's absence.[2]

The next day I perceived that his mind had been directed by her in the same channel not leaving it as was previously determined to Brigham's decision. This circumstance has opened a train of thought that is anything but agreeable. Did I feel that I was to remain with the family by the council of Brigham or even Haywood I would submit with a good grace but as it has been from the source it has, I feel that it is bordering on an interference with my affairs.

The faint probability of going south opened a two-fold gleam of sunlight to lighten my dreary prospect—first my natural inclination for a missionary field and next to enjoy the society of a husband even under the unpleasant circumstances of travelling and apart from this I cannot hope to enjoy this knowledge. Would that my destiny was decided without the responsibility of so doing. Oh how unpleasant is the prospect before me.

On Wednesday evening Mrs. Haywood accompanied Mr. Haywood to Brigham's to have [out] the matter of my coming into the family, but was disappointed in not seeing him. My thoughts and purposes are vacilating continually.

Elder Kimball called here on Monday to express to me his wish that I would withdraw from the Elocution Society, that it might be the means of breaking up the society or drawing away his wives. I was much gratified to him—so good an opportunity of withdrawing—I tendered my resignation on Tuesday evening and was retained an honorary member. Monday evening accompanied Mr. Hall to Mrs. Loetzky in reference to the getting up of a French class.[3] Did not appear to succeed on account of the scarcity of books but yet we do not give up by any means.

January 17th—Friday—Monday evening Brother Brigham and Sister Young spent the evening here with the view of his talking over the subject of Brother Haywood's going south. It was decided that Edgar Blodgett [4] had better accompany Brother Haywood and when the subject of being sealed to him was taken up he said it was all

---

[2] The discussion between the first wife, Sarepta, and the prospective third wife—discreetly carried on during the absence of Mrs. Vary, the second wife—provides some rare insights into plural marriage. Especially noteworthy is Martha's reaction to the idea that she should remain in Salt Lake which she labels as "bordering on an interference with my affairs."

[3] Martha did not intend to wilt on the vine. If she could not be part of the Elocution Society, she would look for other opportunities.

[4] Edgar Blodgett was a younger brother of Sarepta Heywood.

right and of going south it was best not; as the family had best stay together in this place.

When I learned the disposition of my case it seemed to throw such a weight of responsibility on me in taking this step that my feelings were uncommonly oppressed and continued so till the ordinance of sealing was attended to which took place last evening, January 16th, 1851 by Brigham Young in presence of Brother and Sister Vilate Kimball and Thomas Bullock.[5] The ceremony appeared solemn and interesting and different from anything the world knows of. Brother Haywood stood on the floor, his wife taking hold of his left arm with her right and taking first Sister Vary by the right hand and placing it in that of Bro. Haywood's right hand and in that way she was sealed to him for time and eternity by a form of words most sublime. When done she fell back by taking Sister Haywood's arm. I then went forward going through the same ceremony. After this, Brother Young proposed to Brother Kimball giving me a blessing that I felt truly grateful for. It was peculiarly applicable to me. I was to speak in tongues and prophecy, to be a blessing to the lost tribes and to the scattered remnant of Israel. I was to have strength given me for body and mind. The Lord would be merciful to my weaknesses and heal me in body and mind and my faith and prayers in connection with the family should be a blessing to the family. Prosperity should be mine and I should live long on the earth, etc. etc. It was pleasing to witness the free sociable spirit manifested by Brother Brigham and especially during the sealing ordinance his spirit seemed to say—"I am doing a good deed". After his and Brother Bullock's departure we had a social chat with Brother and Sister Kimball not forgetting to speak of Mrs. Hall and Mr. Murray of Rochester.[6] I felt very solemn during the evening. Today I feel a more agreeable feeling, especially a feeling of peace that I have been for some time a stranger to. I feel as if the warfare was over. My destiny has taken its bent and I am satisfied in the man the Lord has given me for a husband.[7]

---

[5] Vilate Murray Kimball, Heber C.'s first wife, was from New York. Thomas Bullock, Salt Lake County recorder, had served as clerk to Joseph Smith and later as chief clerk of the Utah House of Representatives and chief clerk of the LDS Church Historian's Office under Willard Richards and George A. Smith. See Carter, *Our Pioneer Heritage,* 10:384, and Jenson, *LDS Biographical Encyclopedia,* 2:599.

[6] Mrs. Hall was identified earlier by Martha as a sister of Heber C. Kimball. Mr. Murray may have been the father of Vilate Murray Kimball.

[7] This marriage or sealing ordinance would need to be repeated in a somewhat different manner in an endowment house.

January 19th—Sunday—Yesterday went to see Sister Butter-field who is recovering from her severe indisposition. Had a few words with Sarah in reference to her affairs. She still seems inclined to disconnect herself with Brother K. I advised her as well as I could to walk right up to the mark and behave to Brother K. as a wife and then she would realize a very different feeling.[8]

Today attended the Seventies conference which commenced yesterday. Was much interested in what I heard. Brother Brigham made some energetic remarks on the building of the Temple and paying tithing. Said that every man who did not pay tithing should be cut off from the Church. He remarked that endowments would be given long before the Temple was finished as soon as the ground was enclosed, garden walks, beautified fronts and small houses built. Endowments could then be given. He also said that those who got their endowments in Nauvoo did not know much about it. He gave an illustration of how it was by a man being taken in a vision to St. Paul's cathedral in London and when told where he was it closed and finding himself back to his former place, how could he know much about London. And the Saints could tell just as much about their endowments. The apostates have tried to give a description of them over and over again. Brother Kimball spoke in reference to the necessity of a reformation to enable the spirit of this work to go forth with power to ends of the world. He alluded to the endowments given in Kirtland and the power that was felt wherever the gospel was felt. Also when the twelve were in England they asked for the gifts to be poured out on the people and they were manifested at once. In referring to this point he spoke on the connection of the vine and its branches and when the church is right the power will be so great that in part of the world prisons will be not able to keep the brethren. The power of faith will open the prison doors at anytime and it will cause the brethren to say to two mountains to close together to destroy the armies of the enemy as like it was when Moses divided the waters to cause the Saints to flee from their enemies.

Parley P. spoke next and very interesting. After this the Seer was sung by Brother Kay accompanied by Brother Hutchinson and son on their violas. It sounded as well as solo singing could in the Bowery. After the Welsh brethren sang in their native tongue.[9]

[8] How human Martha reveals herself to be. She had been married just a few days and was quite willing to give advice to a dissatisfied wife. Nevertheless, the marriage did not succeed. Sarah Lawrence Kimball divorced Heber C. on June 18, 1851. See Carter, *Our Pioneer Heritage,* 10:413.

[9] This is a good description of a meeting held in a bowery with music that would have sounded much better in a building.

This afternoon did not think it prudent to attend meeting on account of the bad walking and the close atmosphere of the house. I feel sensibly that there is a reformation about to commence and my heart and soul is in it. Last Wednesday evening our weekly prayer meeting was very interesting. Brother Barlow attended and remarked that it was the first prayer meeting he was in. This has been a delightful day like a spring day. Last Thursday night was the coldest night we have had this winter—the night I was united to Brother Haywood in the holy ordinance of sealing and he is now expecting to leave us in six weeks for the South Sea Islands to be gone perhaps two or three years.[10]

January 26th—Sunday—Beautiful weather during the past week, the days very warm and the nights cold. Atmosphere clear and bracing. Last Tuesday evening spent to Brother Parley's. He entertained us with fragments of unfinished literature. One work called the Mysteries of Desseret and another, Old Missouri. Six of his wives were present and the most of them appear to me to be very interesting women. A Scotch girl in particular that has a strong resemblance to my old friend Eliza Ried.[11] Mr. Barlow, as was pre-arranged, visited with us and accompanied me home which gave me the opportunity of talking to him on the subject of my connection with Brother Heywood. He had heard of it but gave it no credence. Said his intention was, the first suitable opportunity to make known to me his wishes. His manly conduct in this matter has elicited my warmest feeling of friendship. The valuable ring he gave me the evening before I was married he requested me to keep as a token of friendship which I most gladly do.[12] I accepted an invitation to a Ball on Friday evening to the Bath house at which I enjoyed myself very much. Wednesday our ward prayer meeting was to Mrs. Pack's. It was a lively good meeting.

Today I enjoyed hearing Brother Parley's speaking on the prophecy relating to the coming forth of the Book of Mormon and its consequence to the American nation. He was followed by Orson

---

[10] A frightening prospect for Heywood's three wives.

[11] Mary Wood Pratt was a native of Glasgow, Scotland. See Reva Stanley, *A Biography of Parley P. Pratt: The Archer of Paradise* (Caldwell, Ida.: Caxton Printers, Ltd., 1937), p. 175.

[12] What a wonderful sensation to learn that another man had been interested in her! The fact that Martha could be escorted by a man other than her husband without causing comment illustrates well the social climate of pioneer Utah.

49

Spencer.[13] I made a call on Mrs. Fanny Murray [14] previous to the meeting—found her in tolerable health but she receives cold whenever she goes out. She remarked that Sister Nancy Green does not enjoy her health at all.

My feelings have been rather calm during the last week though I meet with the little rubs that I anticipated. Tis rather trying to a woman's feelings not to be acknowledged by the man she has given herself to and desires to love with all her heart.[15]

February 2nd—Sunday—Last Monday an express arrived from the Government by the way of California bringing the news of the appointment of the officers of the territory of Utah. Brigham Young, Governor. S. M. Blair, Attorney General. My husband Marshall. This appointment may alter the course of Mr. Haywood's mission to the South Sea Islands—time will tell.[16]

Wednesday evening had a good prayer meeting. Mother Pack sung in tongues and Sister Randall spoke in tongues which was interpreted by Sister Ruth Pack, the first part of which was given to the people that they must be up and doing for great events were about taking place in the church and the latter part was a blessing pronounced on Sister Haywood in reference to Mr. Haywood's going south—that he would gain his health and be blest to the convincing of many of the truths of Jesus—that she should be comfortable in his absence and should have supply to the full for all her wants—that she should be a blessing to many of the daughters of Zion in instructing them in principles and that she should go into another temple, that she should be blest was reitterated many times during the blessing.[17] Brother Hanson gave an interesting description of his travels that pleased me much.

[13] Orson Spencer was chancellor of the University of Deseret and a member of the territorial legislature.

[14] An older sister of Brigham Young.

[15] Heywood was inclined to leave Martha to her own devices much of the time.

[16] Jefferson Hunt, captain of Company A in the Mormon Battalion, had just returned from California on February 2, having led a party of forty-niners there. The overland mail had stopped for the winter; therefore, it was Hunt who brought news from the East via California of Brigham Young's appointment by President Millard Fillmore as governor of the newly created Utah Territory and of the other federal appointments, including Heywood's as federal marshal. Heywood's new position, one of some prestige and many responsibilities, would also give him a cash income and would preclude his going to the South Seas. See Pauline Udall Smith, *Captain Jefferson Hunt of the Mormon Battalion* (Salt Lake City: Nicholas G. Morgan, Sr., Foundation, 1958), pp. 150–62.

[17] Ruth Mosher Pack was the wife of John Pack, a pioneer of 1847. Mother Pack was probably his mother. The Packs lived just west of the Heywoods on

Thursday evening Coln Reese and his sister and sister-in-law spent the evening here. Very uninteresting to me, so much so that I went off to my wagon before they left.

Friday Mr. Woolley's two wives and two children spent the afternoon and evening here. I put my best foot forward to make the time pass pleasantly and I think I succeeded some. Mrs. Anne Woolley seemed very sociable with me and I encouraged the spirit as much as possible.[18] We had expected Bishop Hunter and his family but were disappointed in their not coming.[19]

Saturday afternoon I spent in company with Sisters Haywood and Vary to Sister Crosby's. Sister Savage and Sister Tyrrel were there. We had a very pleasant visit. Mr. Hall has taken up his abode here during the last week—commenced Monday morning.

Today we had a good meeting commenced by Brother Young introducing the subject of Elijah the Prophet and inviting Brother Thomas Bateman to speak in defense of that subject and giving him half an hour.[20] He was scarcely nine minutes. The remarks of Brother Young and Amasa Lyman were very interesting, the former showing who was Elijah and in what way he would come and when and for what purpose.

February 9th—Sunday—During last week I enjoyed my mind pretty well. On Tuesday Mrs. Haywood and I made some calls, principally on Mrs. Hodgekiss, Elder Taylor's first wife and Mrs. Benson.

Wednesday afternoon Sisters Laura, Annie, Christine, Maryann and Ellen Kimball [21] visited with us and we had a very pleasant

the southwest corner of 200 North and West Temple streets. Prayer meetings sometimes took on the atmosphere of the supernatural: speaking in tongues and having the message interpreted. In this case, Sister Pack may have realized the problems Sarepta faced with the prospect of her husband's leaving the valley.

[18] Anne Woolley may have been Mary Ann Alpin whom Edwin D. Woolley had married the previous November. His other wives at this time were Mary Wickersham, Louisa Chapin Gordon, and Ellen Wilding. See Jenson, *LDS Biographical Encyclopedia*, 1:632–33.

[19] The evening seems to have been intended as a reunion of the leaders of the Hunter company of 1850.

[20] Bateman came to Utah in 1850. The "veteran Elder" was accidentally drowned in the Atlantic in 1852 when he was returning from a trip to England. See Jenson, *LDS Biographical Encyclopedia*, 2:591.

[21] These five women were all wives of Heber C. Kimball: Laura Pitkin, known for her spinning and knitting; Ann Alice Gheen, a homebody; Christeen Golden, mother of J. Golden Kimball; Mary Ann Shefflin, known as Mother Shefflin; and Ellen Sanders, one of the three women pioneers who arrived in Salt Lake Valley on July 24, 1847. Heber C. Kimball owned the entire block east of the Heywoods and bounded by Main and State streets and North Temple and 200 North streets which may account for the frequent visits between Kimballs and Heywoods.

interview and in the evening our conversation turned on doctrinal points the result of which seemed to constrain us to say that we were as much edified as if we attended the weekly meeting.[22] Thursday Mr. Haywood was given the word that he was to remain here for the present and prepare for his office. This of course was an agreeable decision for Mrs. Haywood and I feel very well satisfied for the present.

Friday, Mrs. Andrews and Mrs. Brosbie visited us very pleasantly and in the evening we attended the exhibition in which I declined to take any part. It went off well. Saturday Mrs. Oliver Fulmer visited with Mr. Fulmer. Today Seventies meeting in session—commenced yesterday. Brother Lewens has been ordained a seventy. Brother Brigham spoke this afternoon, principally on education and recommends all to go that possibly can.

This afternoon Mr. Haywood spoke followed by Capt. Hunt just came from California. I enjoyed hearing his remarks. He gives a deplorable picture of the society at the mines. Brother Willard Snow made some few remarks, one in particular was in advice to the brethren not to go to law with one another.[23]

Brother and Sister William Snow called to see me today and I enjoyed some conversation with her. I had the pleasure of seeing Brother Stocking.[24] Brother Joel Johnston has removed his family in from the country for the purpose of his contemplated journey to Iron County.[25]

February 16th—Sunday—During the last week we have had quite a storm of snow and cold, but today it is clearing off. Last Tuesday we visited to Sister Horn's in with Sisters Taylor and Stratton, with much pleasure and interests. I enjoyed the company of Sister Taylor very much. During the week I enjoyed my mind

[22] The social life of Salt Lake City in this period consisted largely of neighborly calls just for visiting. These had several general rules: ladies did not call on Monday forenoon. That was wash day. A Tuesday morning call could be excused, for the housewife could visit as she worked. Wednesday, Thursday, and Friday were open days when every woman should be prepared to receive her friends with her house in order, herself dressed in second best (and a dainty waist-apron to quickly exchange for her regular working coverall apron). She must also have something ready to serve.

[23] Willard Snow came to Utah in Jedediah M. Grant's company of 1847. See Jenson, *LDS Biographical Encyclopedia*, 1:574.

[24] John Stocking, his wife Catherine, and their three children, Ensign Israel, Angeline, and Sarah Delight, came to Utah in 1850. See Carter, *Heart Throbs*, 11:447.

[25] Joel Hills Johnson was the elder brother of Joseph Ellis of whom Martha was so fond. Joel and his brother Benjamin F. were both listed as members of George A. Smith's company to settle Little Salt Lake (Parowan), Iron County. See *Deseret News*, November 16, 1850.

pretty well and all seemed pleasant around. I have enjoyed a free spirit and good health and the blessing I received on that night from under the hands of Brother Brigham & Kimball and my husband seems to be coming to pass every day.

Today I had the pleasure of hearing a funeral sermon from Brother Brigham full of light and knowledge, on the death of Sister Noble whose sister Louisa Beman died about a year ago, whose surviving sister is Sister Erastus Snow—the remaining one of three sisters who embraced this work in its infancy and who have adorned their subsequent life by faithfulness.[26] Two of them have finished their work and have gone to the world of spirits and will be crowned with celestial glory in the resurrection. His remarks in reference to all people apart from church was similar to those of Elder Kimball's at Frank's funeral. He gave advice to those who were anxious to know about things in the future, that they had better make the most of what they have got and also to those who were not satisfied with their evidences of being a Mormon, he made some good remarks summed up with the fact that we get just what we are capable of receiving and all that we merit we will get in eternity and to whom little is given there is but little required, but to whom much is given there is much required.

It stormed so fast Wednesday evening that we had no prayer meeting. Our prayer meeting last Sunday evening to Brother Leonard's was full and very good. During last week there were some individuals arrived from the mines among which was William Goddard, Hanna's brother. It seems he has no gold and is going back.

February 23rd—Sunday—On Tuesday we had Mrs. Horn, Mrs. Taylor and Mrs. Stratton to spend the afternoon with us, but Mrs. Haywood was very poorly, having taken cold on Sunday evening previous to prayer meeting but is now better.

The prayer meeting was to Brother Peck's and was crowded very much and almost every one suffered from the confined air. Mr. Haywood received some injury and continued poorly all week. Thursday we had unexpected company, Sister Homisted called in

---

[26] The three sisters were Mary Beman Noble, wife of Joseph B.; Louisa Beman, the first woman to enter plural marriage, being sealed to Joseph Smith on April 5, 1841, by Joseph B. Noble; and Artimesia Beman, first wife of Erastus Snow. See Andrew Karl Larson, *Erastus Snow: The Life of a Missionary and Pioneer for the Early Mormon Church* (Salt Lake City: University of Utah Press, 1971), pp. 235, 736; and Brigham H. Roberts, *A Comprehensive History of the Church of Jesus Christ of Latter-day Saints,* 6 vols. (Salt Lake City: Deseret News Press, 1930), 2:101–2.

and immediately after Mrs. Carington called and was invited with the other Mrs. C.[27] and after they had come Sister Butterfield came. So that we had quite a party. Sister B. stayed all night and next day we made our contemplated visit to Sister Andrews. It stormed very much in the afternoon and evening but we suffered not as we went in a carriage and returned in the same.[28] During the night and following day it stormed a perfect hurricane of snowdrifts and continued to do so till towards evening but today the sun shines very bright and its genial influence is delightful after such a storm, so violent that I never experienced a greater.

As the snow drifts were so great I did not venture to meeting myself but I heard of what was said. Brigham dished up a certain judge who has been laying his plans about going to the president of the States to make a report that the Governor of Utah Territory has so many wives, etc. etc.

March 9th—Sunday—Yesterday I completed my thirty ninth year amongst a new people and in a very new country. For nearly two weeks Mrs. Haywood has been very sick, keeping her bed and in consequence I have taken hold of the housework more extensively which has made me feel very tired and nervous and from this I attribute my not enjoying my mind very well of late.

On Wednesday evening I attended the "Farewell Ball" given to the brethren going South on their various missions. Sister Vary also attended Mrs. Haywood's sickness preventing her. We had a very aggreeable time. Brothers Brigham, Kimball, Benson, Pratt, attended and the first and the last of these made remarks. It did me good to see Brothers Brigham and Benson dance—they were so lively and seemed to enjoy themselves so well. Mr. Haywood enjoyed dancing better than any time previous. We left about twelve o'clock.[29]

Attended meeting today and heard Jedediah Grant, Heber Kimball and Genl. Rich speak but I liked Brother Kimball's remarks best. Brother Brigham spoke this afternoon to the elders.

March 23rd—Sunday—Mrs. Haywood has gained during the last week gradually—was able to attend the wedding of John

[27] Two wives of Albert Carrington, second counselor to Joseph L. Heywood in the bishopric of the Seventeenth Ward and later editor of the *Deseret News* and an apostle. See Jenson, *LDS Biographical Encyclopedia*, 1:126–27.

[28] The social activities of this week were typical of the times: extended calls made just to visit.

[29] The two plural wives had no reason to remain at home just because the first wife was indisposed. The husband would have participated just the same.

Woolley. The party was given to his father's house, of course, in style. The same day I visited to Sister Leonard's and was much pleased with her company. Made out that she and her husband was acquainted with some that I was acquainted with which adds to the interest we feel for one another.

SOME INDICATIONS OF PREGNANCY 6

April 13th—Sunday—Last Sabbath being the 6th of April the Conference was appointed but in consequence of the stormy day was postponed till Monday when it was all done up in one day to the disappointment of many. The principal business done was the appointment of Bishop Hunter to the place vacated by Bishop Whitney's death, as Bishop to the whole Church and Brother Wells, trustee to ————.[1]

Also appointments of several brethren to Iron County and amongst the many going is Mr. Haywood just for the good of his health, to accompany the presidency who are going to visit the settlement.

Today the weather is uncommonly pleasant. Had a good meeting this forenoon. Brother Benson spoke very lengthily and then Brother Brigham followed with divers sermons done up in short order. First, taking the trees and shrubbery from City Creek Canyon, showing the ridiculousness of depriving the water of the creek of its protection from being fouled. Next that of Parley P's canyon which right he sold out to several individuals for his benefit to provide for his expedition and such individual rights ought not be interferred

---

[1] Edward Hunter succeeded Newel K. Whitney as presiding bishop. Daniel Hanmer Wells later served as second counselor to Brigham Young in the First Presidency and filled many civic posts. See Jenson, *LDS Biographical Encyclopedia*, 1:62–66.

with.[2] Another sermon was on the absurd principal of a woman coming to him to know what she must do with her husband; and another sermon was about building a temporary place of worship to be put up this summer on consequence of the unhealthy and uncomfortable state of the present.[3]

Since I last wrote in my journal I have had but poor health. I have reason to think it is in consequence of a change going on in my system giving me some hope of in due time becoming a mother, for which indication I bless the Lord in my inmost soul.

Visited to Mrs. Farr's and Mrs. Stratton's this last week and called to see Mrs. Rosad's three babies born at a birth.[4]

April 20th—Sunday—A steady rain storm during last night and up to this time (noon). Though disappointed in a contemplated good meeting there is a satisfaction in thinking how much advantage this steady rain will be to the wheat and general vegetation. I have sowed a number of flower seeds during this last week commencing on Monday and my one apple and four peach trees are leaved out and looking well. Grape vines show no signs of life as yet which with the others I planted about a month ago or a little over.

On Wednesday attended the Council house to receive my endowment. Sister Buck officiated in the washing and annointing of me and my husband took me through the vail, being the same day (16th) three months, that I was married [5] and expect him to start in two days on his contemplated tour to Little Salt Lake to be gone 6 or 8 weeks. He and Ben Johnston will travel together, to whose family we visited last week. Nature is rapidly growing greener every day. My health has been a little better last week but not so well as I could wish it.

April 27th—Sunday—1851—Mr. Haywood left last Tuesday afternoon for his Salt Lake trip in company with Benjamin Johnston whose health was yet more miserable than Mr. Haywood's. It is to be hoped that they will find what they are after. Alley has recovered her health since he has been gone.[6] Visited to Mrs. Stringam on

[2] Parley P. Pratt had opened the "Golden Pass" road through Parley's Canyon on July 4, 1850, providing travelers with a shortcut to Salt Lake Valley in exchange for a toll of seventy-five cents.

[3] Martha made an excellent resumé of Brigham's brief sermons.

[4] The birth of triplets would have been an unusual event. Martha was probably even more interested in these newborn babies because of her own pregnancy.

[5] Martha's endowment would be a source of comfort and strength to her during her pregnancy and Heywood's absences.

[6] Ally, as she was called, was the four-year-old daughter of Joseph and Sarepta Heywood. She was listed as Alice in the 1850 Census.

Wednesday. I made a call on Mrs. Joseph Young and had a smart discussion on the merits of my choosing a man who had a wife and how much more the first wife had [to] endure than those who voluntary took the men afterwards. This I would not allow. My doctrine is that both have their trials, not alike but one exists as much as the other. Spent Thursday afternoon with Sarah Lawrence where I had another battle with a Mrs. Butterfield, one of the neighbors on the same subject that arose from a remark she made among others that she would not consider a man her husband who had another wife. It seems to me a strange thing to believe Mormonism and not believe or receive the doctrine of plurality of wives as coming from the one source of authority and when the subjects of this principle are not respected on its account then the principle is not.[7] Today we ate for the first time some of our garden produce in the shape of lettuce and pepper grass.

*May 26th—Sunday—*Last evening Mr. Haywood returned rather unexpected and we in the midst of great confusion in consequence of the house undergoing repairs—the foundation having given away during the rain storms. We have had a full supply of rain during the last month which has been unexpected and vegetation has throve under its influence with rapidity. But many have suffered from leaky roofs and some blown off from the great winds. We have been nearly three weeks in perfect muss but have not experienced the calamity of ill health as some have in this place, even to the loss of life. Brother Knowlton lost his youngest daughter very suddenly of three day illness—also Sister Ashby of less than two weeks.

I had the pleasure of receiving a letter from my dear friend Mrs. Strong full of affection and interest and through this medium heard also from Mr. and Mrs. Hayes. That was peculiarly gratifying to me. Mrs. S. is much concerned on the subject of polygamy and requests me to write her the truth and the whole truth.

This afternoon I attended meeting and heard Brigham Young preach an out and outer sermon on gold, merchants, lazy women and men who want nothing but fine clothes—sowing seeds for their own destruction.

*June 8th—Sunday—*For two weeks past I have felt rather miserable in health and some puzzled as to the true cause of it

[7] Although polygamy was practiced in secret and denied in public during the Nauvoo period, it was not yet fully accepted among all the Saints. Not until 1852 would it be declared to all the world as God's "higher law."

having some indications of pregnancy and some rather opposed to it. It tries me a little as to what is the matter with me.[8] Mrs. Haywood has felt pretty weakly for the same time and Sister Vary as usual complaining. But thanks to our Heavenly Father for it, Mr. Haywood has felt well and hearty since his return and seems to enjoy better health than ever I have know him to. His farm speculation seems to gain ground in his mind every day and I feel well pleased with the plan laid out of going there and if it's carried out the Lord will give me wisdom and health for my situation.

Last Sabbath I did not feel able to attend meeting but this afternoon I did and enjoyed the remarks of Joseph Young in reference to keeping the Sabbath holy. Also Brother Kimball in that of not visiting on that day and that of Brigham's in keeping stillness and order during the public services.

Mr. Livingston arrived today from the states and expressed so strong a desire to board here that it has been decided to board him and also others six in numbers when they shall arrive.[9]

I have spent a pleasant hour this afternoon with William Snow's family and attended singing school where I also enjoyed myself. I feel as if I gained a little in strength of voice from the exercise but my secret motive is to have a little exercise of mind during my present state of health of the Lord.

June 15th—Sunday—We have had two exhibitions during the last week. On Tuesday evening Don Cesar *DeBazan* and Dead Shot and on Saturday evening the Stranger and The Gentle Shepard. All went off very well. It fell to [my] lot to make the greater share of the dresses and they looked very well.[10]

Mr. Livingston has been very sick since his arrival and continuing so has had a Doctor Lee from Cottonwood to attend him who boards with us.[11] Mr. L. keeps his bed. By him I have heard that Joseph

[8] This is so typical of Martha's temperament: the desire to know at once and without question.

[9] There were other Livingstons in Salt Lake City, however, later diary references indicate that Martha was referring to the merchant James Monroe Livingston who brought the first stock of goods for the Utah market in 1849 and opened business as a partner in Livingston, Kinkead, & Co.

[10] Although Martha no longer took a leading role in directing the exhibitions, she was largely responsible for the costumes.

[11] Ezekiel Lee, "popularly known as Doctor Lee," was bishop of the Big Cottonwood Ward in the early 1850s. See Francis W. Kirkham and Harold Lundstrom, eds., *Tales of a Triumphant People: A History of Salt Lake County, Utah, 1847–1900* (Salt Lake City: Salt Lake County Company, Daughters of Utah Pioneers, 1947), p. 74. He may also be the Ezekiel Lee, physician, listed as living in the Nineteenth Ward, west of Capitol Hill, by E. L. Sloan, comp., *The Salt Lake City Directory and Business Guide for 1869* (Salt Lake City, 1869), p. 119.

Johnston does not think of coming here this season. This intelligence has since been confirmed by gold emigrants who have arrived during the last week and yet I cannot think it possible that he will not come. A. Babbit has been expected in with his family for the last few days.[12] There is not much gold emigration started from the states this season.

My health has been rather better for two or three days past till today and I again feel poorly. I made out to attend meeting this afternoon, but felt distressed while there—so much so that I could not profit much by which was said. Father Kempton was the first to speak.[13] Major next and then Doctor Richards [14] who spoke on our accountability of receiving instruction when we had opportunity and he also referred to a remark of Father Kempton's that he lived a whole year in Hell and felt that he kept all the commandments. He wished information not conceiving it possible that a person keeping the commandments could have a Hell made for them not even by all the devils in Hell. After the doctor sat down Father Kempton rose and acknowledged the whipping as he called it that the doctor gave but would like to ask him where was Lot when he was in Sodom. The Doctor at once answered "in Hell" which sent quite a lively sensation through the audience.

Had the pleasure of seeing Mr. Lewens able to be out again and looking very well.

June 22nd—Sunday—During last week I felt very poorly indeed but today am better tho weakly and subject to pain. My husband had a long conversation with me last night counselling me to, if possible, assist in the housework sufficient to avoid the hiring of a girl during Mrs. Haywood's expected confinement. I felt as if she did not know how willingly I would enter into the spirit of doing so if I had health and strength to do it. But at all events I am determined to do the best I can and if I am blest with a restoration of comparative health I will do all that lays in my power to be useful to the family for the time I will be with them. I realize that I have

[12] Almon W. Babbitt, Heywood, and John S. Fullmer were in charge of LDS church affairs at Nauvoo after the exodus. Later Babbitt served as secretary of Utah Territory. Martha's interest in the Babbitts may have stemmed from an acquaintance with his wife Julia Ann Johnson Babbitt, an elder sister of Joseph Ellis Johnson.

[13] This was probably John Kempton, a member of the High Council of Salt Lake Stake, 1849–52. See Lynn M. Hilton, ed., *The Story of the Salt Lake Stake, 1847–1972* (Salt Lake City: Salt Lake Stake, Church of Jesus Christ of Latter-day Saints, 1972), p. 298.

[14] Dr. Willard Richards, second counselor to Brigham Young from 1847 to 1854, filled a large number of church and civic posts. See Jenson, *LDS Biographical Encyclopedia,* 1:53–56.

both a good and a kind husband to look to and to trust in and I hope I may yet be able to prove to him that I realize this. The repairs of the house are now about finished and I believe we shall all feel better of it. Mr. Livingston is recovered sufficient to come to his meals again, having commenced this noon in so doing.

Attended meeting this forenoon and heard some good speaking from the brethren but particularly from Brigham Young. He spoke very warmly of the Church store being abused and especially by the sisters and in connection with this matter he alluded to how little tithing was sent in and how much was expended on public improvement.

June 29th—Sunday—An eastern mail arrived last evening. No news of any importance. Heard that A. W. Babbit left with the Government officers the 16th of M.—Kanesville.

On Friday Brother and Sister Blair visited with us in company with Judge Brandenbury, our new officer.[15] Mother Snow happened in during the day and she also spent the afternoon. I should have enjoyed the visit but for a violent bowel complaint that came quite sudden and prostrated me for the rest of the day. I had a little visit with Mother Snow and enjoyed it well.

July 6th—Sunday—Had a delightful 4th of July excursion in the form of a trip to Salt Lake where I enjoyed myself in the ride, exercises on the ground and the bathing.[16] Returned much better in health about two o'clock yesterday and rode to the warm springs and bathed there for the first time and today I feel better than I have for the last few months—so much so that I have attended meeting all day, visited to Brother Snow's and attended singing school. Had most excellent preaching in the forenoon from Father Cahoon,[17] Father Kempton and Brother Brigham, the burden of whose remarks were that *constituted,* Hell was "wanting to do it and couldn't". This afternoon Thomas Bullock, Brother Felt and Brother Kimball.

[15] Lemuel G. Brandcbury was named chief justice of Utah in 1850 and would therefore have been associated with Joseph L. Heywood, the new U. S. marshal, and Seth M. Blair, U. S. attorney. The Blairs were no doubt introducing the judge to the city's society. See Tullidge, *History of Salt Lake City,* p. 78.

[16] Many Salt Lakers celebrated the July 4 holiday by taking an excursion to Black Rock, Great Salt Lake. See Andrew Jenson, comp., *Church Chronology* (Salt Lake City, 1914), p. 43.

[17] Reynolds Cahoon came to Salt Lake City in 1848. Born April 30, 1790, at Cambridge, N. Y., he joined the LDS church on October 12, 1830, and was for years closely associated with Joseph Smith. At Far West he served under David Patten of the Danite band. He settled in Murray, Utah, where he died April 29, 1861. See Stella Cahoon Shurtleff and Brent F. Cahoon, *Reynolds Cahoon and His Stalwart Sons* (Salt Lake City, 1960).

July 13th—Sunday—Moon changed yesterday which brought us a delightful shower today,[18] the first rain we have had for several weeks. Last Sunday I felt so well that I supposed I was about having better health, but from walking too much or something else on Wednesday I flattened down again. Sister Susanna Richards called here on that day and having consulted her she told me what it was that caused my pains and prescribed for me. It has been a relief to my mind to have some little knowledge of what the matter was with me. Time seems to confirm my suppositions of being pregnant for which I feel grateful to my father in heaven and willingly will bear the trials consequent to it tho this is not connected with the pains and distress that I suffer so much from. Oh may the Lord give me strength to bear and bring forth a child in this my advanced age, and to his service will I dedicate it with all my heart and soul.

Mr. Livingston's brother arrived here on Thursday, 10th, and was here to supper. He is an interesting appearing young man and very sociable.

Ruth Kimball [19] had her confinement this night, a little girl who died or was dead on coming into this world. This calamity was very unexpected as the mother was so uncommonly well all the time of her pregnancy. Mrs. Haywood to our great surprise still keeps about.

July 20th—Sunday—On Tuesday the 15th between 12 and 1:00 o'clock Mrs. Haywood was safely delivered of a daughter and both have been doing very well since. The babe is very sweet and interesting and I think will favor her mother more than Alice does. She is a lively interesting good baby and already I love it very much. Mrs. H. was about four hours in labor.

Yesterday the 19th Alman Babbit arrived. He brought me a letter from Joseph E. Johnston who writes me that he is not coming this year and wishes me to send on some money by the return of Mr. Babbit and also that he sends me a stock of cap materials.[20] May the Lord bless him in his afflictions as he seems to be wading through them in pecuniary affairs. Mother Johnston is well but not coming for which I am very sorry, as also Mrs. Therman. It seems hard to me that Mr. B. would come without them but Mrs. Carter and others of his family are on the way as also Mrs. Snider's.

[18] An item of folklore from the period.

[19] Ruth Reese Kimball, wife of Heber C. and sister of John and Enoch Reese. The infant Susannah was one of some fifty-six persons buried in the Kimball-Whitney Cemetery on Gordon Place between Main and State streets. See Carter, *Our Pioneer Heritage,* 10:392–93, 427.

[20] A stock of cap materials would be most welcome, for Martha would probably get better quality at a lower price from Johnson.

Zerubbabel Snow, Mr. Snow, etc. Government officers came with Mr. Babbit. They had much rain by the way which caused them delay and serious damage.[21]

Mr. Livingston's first train of goods came in during last week. His goods are of the first quality.

August 3rd—Sunday—Mrs. Haywood has gained as well as could be expected for her and now about the house and able to wait on herself. The baby has been very healthy but troubled some with colic—grows very fast. She is named "Sarah Idoo". My health is not very good—weather warm and my situation makes me feel miserable all the time. Did not exercise very much last week but sewed steady.

Spent Wednesday afternoon to Mrs. Butterfield's to visit Mrs. Sindy[?]. Did not find her very interesting. Some like her daughter but make out to learn something of the folks back. Did not attend meeting today but learned that Doctor Bernhisel spoke of his travels very interestingly this forenoon and Brother Brigham this afternoon. Brother Babbit is expected to speak next Sabbath forenoon. Reports of the cholera raging East and at the mines and high water destruction.

Mr. Livingston started this morning to meet Mr. Kinkaid.[22]

Mr. Haywood's health has been poorly for three or four weeks and I believe it will not be better till he makes his trip to Salt Creek.

The last mail brought nothing for me. I feel confident that letters have been written but gone astray.[23]

[21] "Four of the newly appointed Federal officers for Utah, namely, Judge Zerubbabel Snow, Secretary Benjamin D. Harris and Indian Agents Stephen B. Rose and Henry R. Day arrived in G.S.L. City, accomplished by Dr. John M. Bernhisel and Almon W. Babbitt." Jenson, *Church Chronology*, 43. Bernhisel became Utah's first delegate to Congress on August 4, 1851, when the new territory's first general election was held. See Jenson, *LDS Biographical Encyclopedia*, 1:724. Zerubbabel, a brother of Erastus Snow, was one of two associate justices of the territorial supreme court.

[22] Kinkaid (sometimes spelled Kincaid or Kinkade) was Charles A. Kinkead of Livingston, Kinkead & Co. For an interesting glimpse of pioneer merchandising see Kinkead's sworn testimony given before a Washington, D.C., justice of the peace in July 1856 in J. Cecil Alter, *Utah, the Storied Domain*, 3 vols. (Chicago and New York: American Historical Society, 1932), 1:217.

[23] Martha refused to think that her friends just might have forgotten to write or been too busy. Her trust in the enduring ties of friendships is cheering.

*September 21st—Sunday—*Started from the city on Wednesday (17th) afternoon, one o'clock in company with my husband and his nephew for the new settlement of Salt Creek with bouyant spirits and hope in full exercise.[1] Wagon load of necessaries, our span of mares in good order, dog sharp and little kitty to bring up the rear. Also cow and calf but had to leave the calf at Willow Creek. The first night we put up to Brother Smoot's at Little Cottonwood, 10 miles from the City.[2] Started from there about ten o'clock in the forenoon—nooned at Willow Creek where we left the calf in the care of Brother Brown.[3] Tarried for the night with Brother McLellan's folks, camp fashion, after we passed the point of the mountain, on entering Utah Valley the scenery of which was splendid. Started about ten next morning and moved to Brother Harrington's, American Fork, where we had a most excellent dinner for ourselves

[1] Salt Creek, so named because of some salt springs in a nearby canyon that fed the stream, was laid out on the lower slopes of Mount Nebo. The town was later renamed Nephi in honor of a Book of Mormon patriarch. The county seat of Juab County, Nephi was a stopping place on the main route to southern California. By the end of 1851 the settlement had twenty-three cabins, chiefly of willows and mud. See Roberts, *Comprehensive History,* 3:480.

[2] They had evidently stopped at the home of Abraham O. Smoot who became prominent as mayor of Salt Lake City and, later, of Provo.

[3] Ebenezer and Phoebe Brown, who had settled in the Draper area, raised and fattened cattle to sell to emigrants on the way to the gold fields. See Kirkham and Lundstrom, *Tales of a Triumphant People,* p. 228.

and animals.[4] Started from there about half past two and reached Provo a little after sundown where we tarried for the night alone. Made our own breakfast and started at seven, arrived about eleven to Sister Pine's at Hobble Creek [5] who with her family were delighted to see us. Made us a hasty dinner and supplied us liberally with squashes, pumpkins, beets, watermelon, etc. Arrived here last evening to Brother McLellan's house, he not here Mrs. Mc. did the honors of the house most hospitably.[6] Today we have enjoyed ourselves in this place attending meeting and visiting around. Theodore has suffered all day with the earache receiving cold last night in consequence of a rain storm that wet his bedding in the waggon. (At Petit Neat)

Salt Creek Settlement—September 23rd—Wednesday—Arrived here on Monday evening at half past six o'clock. Found the brethren on the ground in good spirits—delighted with the valley, had some carralls made. Brother Baxter [7] invited us to supper of which we partook and immediately after Mr. Haywood called a meeting to commence the organization of the people. Meeting opened by Father Gifford [8] after which Mr. Haywood made some appropriate remarks in reference to the necessity of having a watch as the little property we had in cattle and horses was our all and could not be very well risked and by strictly guarding the settlement in this way it might save a great deal of trouble with the Indians. He called for an expression of the brethren on the subject a few of which spoke in favor of establishing the watch, whereupon a vote was taken and also a vote appointing Brother Foote the captain of the guard and also to have an oversight in reference to the brethren having fire arms and in good order with the privilege of calling them out for examination and drill when he thinks suitable.[9] Next Mr. H. pro-

[4] Leonard E. Harrington, a former neighbor, was the first bishop of American Fork. See Jenson, *LDS Biographical Encyclopedia*, 3:799–800.

[5] Hobble Creek was renamed Springville.

[6] The Heywood party seems to have arrived at the settlement on Peteetneet Creek now known as Payson. Brother McLellan may have been James or William C. McClellan, early settlers in the area. See Emma N. Huff, comp., *Memories That Live: Utah County Centennial History* (Springville, Ut.: Utah County Company, Daughters of Utah Pioneers, 1947), pp. 434–35, 438.

[7] Zimri H. Baxter, one of the first Nephi settlers, had been active in the work on the Nauvoo Temple.

[8] This was probably Levi Gifford, one of the first Nephi settlers. Levi and his son Ichabod both served as town councilors. See Alice Paxman McCune, *History of Juab County, 1847–1947* (Nephi, Ut.: Juab County Company, Daughters of Utah Pioneers, 1947), pp. 56, 61.

[9] Timothy Bradley Foote reportedly built the first home in Salt Creek, and he was one of the town's first aldermen. Ibid., pp. 59, 61. Foote's name appears

posed Father Gifford to preside over the meetings who was accordingly voted. Mr. H. also made some observations as to the right of individuals taking up and following their own particular branch of business and counseled Br. Baxter to build a grist mill and Brother Camp [10] to build a saw mill. Meeting was closed by prayer by Brother Foote.

Tuesday we all enjoyed ourselves as new settlers remarkably well and the more the brethren explored the ground the better pleased they were. In the afternoon I walked about one half mile up the creek to see where we would have our lot and we were delighted with the place we design having our lot or lots, as Mr. H. will take more than he wants for himself as some of his friends may come on and he would be glad to have a place for them. That portion of the creek that we desire is beautifully adorned with trees according to my heart's desire. In the evening, meeting was convened and Father Gifford as president opened the meeting by calling on Brother Miller to pray. Mr. H. remarked that we might have some singing which was heartily agreed and we sung unitedly "Come Let us Anew", after which Mr. H. made a few remarks about the guard and proceeded to take the names which were accordingly.

Wednesday Mr. H. in company with Brother Camp started to explore the canyon where salt is to be obtained and immediately after his starting Brother Fox arrived with word that the Presidency were obliged to give up their intended trip to this place in consequence of the legislature being called and that Brigham sent word to Mr. H. to do the best he could in laying out the city.[11] A reminiscence of our former acquaintance as travelling companions served to wile away the afternoon with Brother Fox and I as Mr. H. did not return till dark, much later than anticipated which caused me some little uneasiness, fearing that they had missed their road. Also a man arrived from the city of Benjamin Johnston, with a note to Mr. H. requesting him to provide the man with board until a wagon comes

frequently in Mormon history. He was a captain of the captains of ten in the second fifty of the 1848 immigration. Foote was one of several men who crossed paths with the dubious Dr. J. M. Vaughan, an accused adulterer who was shot and killed earlier in 1851. For details of this story see Brooks, *On the Mormon Frontier,* 2 : 380–81, 393, 396.

[10] This was probably William Camp, a blacksmith from Georgia, who was listed in the 1850 Census as residing in Davis County. Camp was involved in court action over his Black slave, Dan, in 1856. See Brooks, *On the Mormon Frontier,* 2 : 597.

[11] Jesse W. Fox accompanied Brigham Young on many of his trips to locate cities throughout the territory. Fox succeeded William Lemmons as surveyor of Salt Lake City and was later surveyor-general of Utah. He also taught school in Manti. See Jenson, *LDS Biographical Encyclopedia,* 1 : 774–75.

with provisions and also to direct him in cutting hay, etc. until he heard further.[12] This and Brother Fox having to board with us, Brother Camp having already done so since his being here, makes three boarders and with us three makes quite a family to cook for to a new beginner in housekeeping but as I have often remarked that "as my days so shall my strength be" and so it is. My health is much better than in the city and my aptness for cooking comes with the necessity and this I always believed in.

Thursday—This morning the brethren convened together for the purpose of taking into consideration the laying of the city. The following was agreed to—that the blocks be 26 rods square, each block containing 4 lots and the streets 6 rods wide with the exception of the state road passing north and south which will be 8 rods wide, two blocks square to be reserved out of the same reserved for public purposes. The city to be 8 blocks square.

September 28th—The brethren after convening for a short meeting session started to explore the canyons in search of building timber, leaving Brother Fox to have a care of us women. Returned late in the afternoon bringing good reports of plenty of timber but inaccessible to hewing for the present. Had a meeting and this was the principle subject discussed. Brethren Camp and Gifford started for the city this morning. I did not feel very smart today and did but little but yet my health seems to gradually improve and Mr. H. is remarkably good.

October 3rd—Friday—Monday morning Brother Baxter started in company with one of the Gifford boys for the canyons to get out some house logs and remain one or more nights. Tuesday Mr. H. and Brother Fox with Theodore started for Sanpete to get lumber and a wagon box made. Also Brother Miller with his company started for the city to be there in time for Conference, so that we had but two men and three boys left to take care of us women folks if the Indians should happen this way. Towards night the mail

---

[12] Benjamin F. Johnson had not, after all, gone with George A. Smith to settle Parowan, probably because of an accidental injury. In the spring of 1851 he accompanied Brigham Young on an exploring trip "up the Sevier, and over the mountains into Iron County. . . . Brother Joseph L. Heywood assisted in providing a team . . . we camped at Summit Creek (Santaquin) in Utah County. . . . It appeared to me as enchanted ground. . . . President Young heard me and asked if I would like to settle a colony there, and I said, 'yes,' if he wished me to. He said he did, and that I might commence my arrangements as soon as I returned." See Benjamin F. Johnson, *My Life's Review* (Independence, Mo.: Zion's Printing and Publishing Company, 1947), pp. 132, 135.

carrier arrived which strengthened our party. Wednesday night Brother and Sister Billings with her niece, Mrs. Kimball and their son called, by Mr. H.'s request, on their way to Conference.[13] I found Mrs. Billings to be a very motherly agreeable woman. Mrs. Kimball who is Father Morley's daughter slept with me so that I had quite an acquaintance with her.

Last evening Mr. H. returned from San Pete bringing with him Mrs. Noble and child.[14] Started this morning with her for the city leaving me to try the friendship of this little community in his absence. Immediately after it commenced raining and continued all day, wind blowing at times very violently which made it very unpleasant about cooking and quite cold sitting in the wagon.

October 4th—Saturday—This morning Brother Fox and the mail carrier returned from San Pete having spent the night in the canyons with six mules as the mares suffered so much in travelling the wet roads. They also had to leave the lumber ten miles this side of San Pete. About noon when Theodore went after the mares to prepare to start for the city he found one of the mares (Palmer) had lost her colt in consequence of the hard day's travel the day before. So we concluded it would not answer to put her in harness in her weak state.

October 10th—Friday—Sunday the 5th Palmer was so much better as to be able to travel so that Theodore and the mail carrier started about noon with the horses and wagon for the city. I thought I should then have a resting spell for a season but was mistaken. After taking a walk to where our lot is, which fatigued me very much, a team arrived with Mary Anne (B. Johnston's wife) and child and the teamster Ezra B. ———. I was so glad to see her that it excited me very much and flew about without any feeling but that of joy which caused me a night's suffering afterwards. Brother Baxter attempted to have a meeting [in] the evening but it proved rather a failure. He proposed having the next on Thursday evening. I suggested that we might have it on Tuesday evening to which he assented and we separated. The day was very pleasant.

Monday was pleasant weather and I verily thought that Sister Johnston's arrival would rid me of all responsibility in the house

---

[13] The party of travelers would appear to have been settlers from Manti on their way to the semiannual October conference of the LDS church in Salt Lake City. The group probably included Titus and Diantha Billings. A Brigham Kimball, age seven, was listed as living with the Billings family at Manti in the 1850 Census, but whether this was the son of Mrs. Billings's niece is not known.

[14] Probably a wife of Joseph Bates Noble.

keeping department but between the confusion of her things and her little boy not feeling very well I found I had to do about as much as ever—all the extra time I worked on the awning, hoping to have a kind of shed to screen us from the weather. After considerable labor on the part of James and myself we raised it over the two wagons but for want of more cross poles on [the] back part I did not think it very safe.

Tuesday—Rather stormy looking. Helped Mary Anne some to fix her things in the forenoon, and in the work, that she might have a chance to get her things fixed. In the afternoon made her an apron and commenced a warm sack to keep her boy warm who seemed to suffer much from the cold air morning and evenings. The afternoon was turned out very stormy and very cold. Our awning covering was blown down by the hard wind.

Wednesday—Looked as if it might clear off. Had my washing done with Sister Margaret Baxter's assistance. Felt rather tired in the afternoon, made out to finish the little boy's sack. Quite stormy all the afternoon and snowed before we retired.

Thursday—Snowed during the night so that there was quite a surface on everything about two inches deep on the tops of the waggons but not quite so cold. The sun kept in clouds all the forenoon, the ground very wet and air chilly. About noon the sun came out very shy. I wrung out my clothes out of the cold water and shortly after was taken with a bowel complaint which obliged me to go to bed which prevented me from accomplishing anything. I felt some better in the evening and attended the meeting which was made interesting by the arrival here of a Brother Klingonsmith from the city on his way to San Pete, who gave us considerable news concerning the conference of a very cheering nature.[15] The principle business was the making [of] settlements all along the southern route.

This day the sun came out with considerable vigor but in the shade was very cold. Made two caps for Sister Margaret's boys. Brother Morley [16] passed here this afternoon—had some refreshment at Brother Baxter's, told them that Brother George A's company would be here in a few days and [it] was expected that Mr. H.

[15] In 1851 Philip Klingensmith was in the bloom of manhood: tall, handsome, keen of mind, and a confirmed optimist. He and his family were living in Manti. In a few years he would participate in the massacre at the Mountain Meadow. Klingensmith was the first to break the pledge of silence, making his deposition before the county clerk in Delamar, Nevada. His story was essentially the same as that told many years later by other participants.

[16] Isaac Morley, frequently called Father Morley, had taken charge of the company that settled Sanpete valley in the fall of 1849. He had served as first

would be along with the next company which would be for this place.

October 12th—Sunday—Yesterday pleasant and rather warmer than the day before. Made out to commence my cloth caps but did not work to much advantage on account of the cold air which affects my health, giving me the bowel complaint several times within the last few days but good health is general among our little company and peace and good will with the exception of Brother Baxter's family who are disagreed among themselves.

Today has been some warmer than yesterday and I have been better in health. This evening according to appointment we met together for worship and had a good meeting. Br. Baxter called on Brother Foote to pray after the meeting had been opened by singing. The remarks made by Bro. F. and B. were excellent. Sister Gifford spoke a few words and I followed her, feeling a desire to acknowledge the goodness of the Lord to me all the day long.

October 13th—Monday—Very pleasant weather. James and Ezra hauled two loads of hay. I worked on my caps all day. Mrs. Johnston's little boy improves in health. Two or three straggling Indians round. We all enjoy ourselves first rate with the exception of Brother Baxter's two wives who are determined to leave him.

Tuesday—Warm pleasant day. The nights and mornings are very cold. Expected that Ezra would have started early this morning after the lumber but it took him so long to go after the cattle that it was near noon before he started. James cut hay all day. The mail carrier arrived in the evening bringing intelligence of a company near at hand on their way to Salt Lake. Heard nothing from Mr. H. or B. Johnston.

Wednesday—Still continues pleasant weather. This morning the cattle returned that Ezra took yesterday morning. Expect they have been on the road all night from where he camped. The mail carrier fortunately about starting, drives them back but makes yesterday's work on Ezra's part worse than nothing.

October 16—Thursday—Very pleasant weather. Last evening ten wagons arrived here on their way to [Little] Salt Lake or Iron County and this morning Brother John Smith came over from the

counselor to Bishop Edward Partridge from 1831 to 1840 and had been ordained a patriarch in 1838. From 1851 to 1857 he served in the territorial legislative council, representing Sanpete County. See Jenson, *LDS Biographical Encyclopedia,* 1:235–36.

camp to see me.[17] Had no word from Mr. H. but learned that the Presidency was coming this way to locate the capital in Pauvan Valley.[18] Said we might expect them the first of the week. Suffered some today from bowel complaint—have it more or less lately. Otherwise my health is good. Making some progress with my cap work. A Brother Everett of San Pete ordered two caps from me today.[19] Sent Brother Washburn's by him and I sent Br. Patten's by the mail carrier yesterday.

October 17th—Friday—Brother Foote started this morning for the city. I sent by him a cap for Brother Barlow and one for Betty Johnson's little boy. Brother Foote expected to meet Mr. H. on the way. A party of Californians camped here last night. Weather very pleasant during sunshine but very cold night and morning.

Our prayer meeting last was a kind of confession meeting, more particularly on the part of Brother Baxter who feels pretty bad about the girls going away. Felt rather poorly today.

October 18th—Saturday—Still pleasant weather. Joel Johnston's family arrived here this afternoon in company with other wagons on their way to Salt Lake. They made some little excitement and confusion for Mary Anne and I. The children were so cross and noisy.

October 19th—Sunday—Pleasant day, rather cloudy in the afternoon. Walked up to our lots with Mary Anne which hurt me some. She was much pleased with the location but rather disappointed to find that her lot did not join mine, Brother Fox's being between. Joel's folks started after breakfast and we were glad of it. They made so much confusion. This afternoon Brother Bradley and family came from the city, not bringing me a single word from Mr. H. They will start in the morning for San Pete—he will return immediately to get his house. Also Father Gifford arrived from the city and still no word from Mr. H. or any other news. Our prayer meeting did not amount to much, was late on Father Gifford's account.

Tuesday night—When the mail carrier arrived this evening bringing no intelligence excepting that no one had started for this place up to Monday morning, it made me quite low spirited, together with not feeling very well, a sort of melancholy came over me

[17] This was John Calvin Lazelle Smith of Parowan.

[18] The territorial capital was to be located in Pauvan or Pahvant Valley, present-day Fillmore, Millard County.

[19] This was probably Elijah (or Elisha) Everett rather than Addison Everett, the former being listed in the 1850 Census as a resident of Manti.

that I could not shake off. John D. Lee and Company arrived today bound for the further settlement on the rim of the basin.[20]
Brother Gustin, etc. arrived here from San Pete but are going to the
city before stopping here.[21]

October 21st—Wednesday—This morning Sister Morley passed
on her way to the city. Sent Mrs. Benson's cap by her. She had an
order from Morley to get pay for the lumber that Mr. H. got from
Shumways that was given by mistake. She wants a cap made and
will send the size.

Bishop Call's company for Pauvan [22] settlement arrived today
on their way—about 15 wagons making with Brother Lee's over
thirty wagons camping tonight on the other side of the creek—so
that almost every night we have an addition to our number, more
or less. James and Ezra finished getting up the hay today as too late
to cut anymore.

October 22nd—Thursday—The two companies started this
forenoon for their respective destines. Also Brother Gustin and those
who came with him, for the city and with them started also Father
Gifford. Sister Margaret and her two boys and Liddy, the wives
of Brother Baxter who are determined to leave him as they consider
they have not been properly treated either by him or Sister Baxter.
As a company we are very few indeed, there being only 2 men, 4
women, 5 boys and three children. If the Indians were known to
this our cattle would be in danger. Two of Brother Call's wagons
happened along this evening which was very pleasing to me at least
for the name of having more.

October 23rd—Friday—Another company of twelve wagons
arrived today about noon from Pauvan and with the two camp on
the other side of the creek. This evening Brigham and his company
arrived on their way to Pauvan.[23] He and Brother Kimball spent

[20] John D. Lee had served as official recorder for the Iron County Mission
of 1850–51. At the October 1851 LDS church conference he was authorized to
start a settlement at the junction of the Rio Virgin and Santa Clara River. For
details of this venture see Robert Glass Cleland and Juanita Brooks, eds., *A
Mormon Chronicle: The Diaries of John D. Lee, 1848–1876*, 2 vols. (San
Marino, Calif., Huntington Library, 1955), 1:133–34.

[21] This was probably Amos Gustin (listed as a Manti resident in the 1850
Census), who was named one of nine councilors in the first election at Nephi
in May 1852. See McCune, *History of Juab County*, p. 61.

[22] Anson Call, an early settler in Davis County, had been authorized by
the legislative assembly to organize Millard County. See Roberts, *Comprehensive
History*, 4:10 n. 18.

[23] On October 21, 1851, Brigham Young, Heber C. Kimball, George A.
Smith, Zerubbabel Snow, Daniel H. Wells, Major Rose (Indian subagent), and

some of the evening with us. Also Brothers George A., Horace Eldridge, Fox, etc. So that we had a very pleasant evening. Had a letter from Mr. H. who expects to be here in a few days. Benjamin Johnston has got as far as Summit Creek and will be here tomorrow. Heard from Brother Fox that Theodore has again run away which will cripple Mr. H. very much. Sister Vilate Kimball has sent me cloth, etc. to make caps for her boys and to use Brother Kimball's words, sends me lots of love.

October 25th—Sunday—Last evening Brother Benjamin Johnston arrived to our great joy and satisfaction. It seemed to me about as good as Mr. Haywood's coming himself, tho he came with an idea of taking his family back to Summit Creek, supposing that little or nothing was done here for his benefit. He readily admitted that his men had done well and was delighted to find his boy looking so much better than when he left the city. He is of the same opinion with Mary Anne and myself that it would be every way more economical and pleasant for us to live together this winter and has given directions to the men to build a willow house as quick as possible. Was disappointed that our lots were not side by side and concluded to risk having the house put up on Brother Fox's lot which comes between ours. He is very willing to have Ezra leave him and hire to Brother Baxter or anyone else. I received by him a letter and parcel from Mr. H. and further intelligence that Mr. H. would not be here before the first of the month which knowledge more forcibly determining me to fall in with theirs and my own wishes to live with Mary Anne.

Mary Anne and I had a pleasant ride today to see and determine about the lots and also to the Plaster Paris mountain.[24] Brother B. [Benjamin Johnson] is much pleased with this place and appears to be well satisfied that he has made a start here. He has James consent to remain with him and take up land to make him a farm.

others left Salt Lake City for the Pauvan Valley. They traveled through Utah and Juab counties and reached Chalk Creek in Pauvan Valley on October 28. On the following day a site was selected for the territorial capital and surveyed. The city was named Fillmore and the county Millard after the president. See *Deseret News,* November 29, 1851. A daily account of the journey was printed in the *News* on December 13, 1851. This was an important event in the history of Utah Territory. Perhaps because of it, Governor Young proclaimed January 1, 1852, "A Day of Praise and Thanksgiving" for the territory and asked his followers to wash their bodies with pure water, attend to their flocks and herds, prepare the "best of food," and abstain from evil thoughts, words, and deeds. See *Deseret News,* December 27, 1851.

[24] Gypsum of the massive rock variety was abundant in a nearby canyon and later proved to be an important resource for the county when it was commercially mined.

Our company has no additions as yet but are all well and meet [with] no disturbance. Brother Baxter for some reason best known to himself* has avoided speaking to me since the girls went away. I presume I shall find out the reason in due time. I have no considerable cap work to attend to as Brother Benjamin has brought me some material to make him some for his men and boys and also will trade as many caps as I can make for the things that I will want.

LITTLE DIFFICULTIES 8

January 1st, 1852—It is now over two months since making any record, in which time my darling boy was born on the 18th of Nov. about half past nine forenoon in the wagon.[1] Was first taken sick on the night of the 15th. Suffered much unnecessary pain and distress from taking a wrong position as also from the smallness of the wagon and its openness. Sister Anna Gifford was all the assistance I had and after my sweet one was born was left pretty much to myself, having taken all the care of my babe from the time he was first dressed.

January 4th—Sunday—Two weeks yesterday since my husband left here for the city, having stopped over night on his way to and from San Pete and since then I have suffered much from bowel complaint but feel better the last few days. Mary Anne has been to Summit Creek since the day after Christmas and in consequence

[1] Joseph Neal Heywood, the first of two children born to Martha Spence and Joseph L. Heywood, filled an LDS church mission to New Zealand in 1888–91; served as bishop of the Alpine Ward, Saint John's Stake, Arizona, 1891–96; and was a schoolteacher like his mother and a farmer. Neal and his wife, Sarah Francelle Coleman, had eleven children. He died in 1904. See Jenson, *LDS Biographical Encyclopedia*, 4:597. Additional information was obtained from family genealogical records.

From this point on in the diary, Martha more frequently spells the names Heywood and Johnson correctly rather than as Haywood and Johnston. Perhaps she was seeing the names written out more frequently since much of her communication with Heywood and members of the Johnson family was through the mails. Therefore, regardless of the way they appear in the typescript, both names have made to conform henceforth.

I have to see much to the cooking which prevents me as yet seeing much to the cap trade. I have about 25 orders to fill and it worries me to think I have not been able to do some of them. But my dear little boy is in good health and very hardy and to this day has not had an hour's sickness and now being over six weeks old he can laugh and appears to enjoy himself which makes him such company for me.

Our settlement here progressed very well. The public carrell is about finished—there are 18 houses, most of them logs, 3 adobies.[2] The brethren are, in general, the right kind of men for a new settlement and with a little exception they are united in efforts to build up the place. I am more and more satisfied with the location I have chosen in the place and hope in due time to occupy my lot with a good log house on it.

January 11, 1852—Sunday—Last Wednesday Sister Mary Anne returned from Summit Creek and by her return the knowledge of a little difficulty between her and her husband that arose from a conversation between Harriet and I when she was here at Christmas that caused me much pain. But having [written?] to Benjamin about it I feel easier about it and have realized that it will in all probability produce good where most desired and if so I can well afford to bear the stigma, knowing that I am [free] of any evil intentions in the matter.

I enjoy day by day my sweet babe and find that in possessing him my cup is full, such as it has not been before and I am willing to bear some little difficulties in the possession of him.

Have not heard from Mr. Heywood for more than —— but when I last heard he was very well and all the family.

There is general health in this place and peace and unity as far as I learn. Today meeting to Bro. Bradley's,[3] the brethren have projected the getting up of a school house and arranged to finish the bridges. The weather has been uncommonly warm during the last week. More so than I realized in the city last year about this time.

(Night) I received a letter this evening from both Mr. and Mrs. Heywood full of concern and affectionate regard for my health as also that I have been remembered in the prayer circle. May the

[2] Compare this with Joseph L. Heywood's letter to the *Deseret News*, December 13, 1851, which says that twelve homes had been built: three adobies, two of willows plastered inside and out, a two-story house of four-inch plank, and the remainder of logs.

[3] Probably George W. Bradley, an early settler in Nephi. See McCune, *History of Juab County,* p. 56.

Lord grant me wisdom to appreciate all the blessings I am surrounded with and also do the right thing to preserve my health.

January 16th—Friday—This night completed one year of my becoming a married woman, the result of which is my coming into possession of my precious boy who lacks two days of being two months old and having a husband to care and watch over me that I feel reverance, love and esteem [for] and connected with a family that I am proud to be a member of, and realize that I am much happier now than I was a year ago. My child is the consummation of all my earthly wishes.

January 25th—Sunday—Attended meeting today as also the last Sabbath, both of which I enjoyed very much. Have gained in my health much during last week. Have not heard lately from Mr. H. My boy seems to grow nicely tho troubled with colic some and very nervous.

February 18th—Wednesday—Today my baby has completed three months of its sojourn here which is a great comfort to me, having had the greatest anxiety from the day of its birth to this period and shall now have more hope of its being left with me as it has gained this period. I made out to invite some of my neighbors to spend the afternoon with me as I have received much kindness from them in the way of hospitality. I thought I would take advantage of the first opportunities I felt able to entertain them as Mary Anne never seemed disposed to have any of our neighbors to come to us and my health so miserable I could not have any over to spend an afternoon till now. I had Sisters Bradley, Gustin, Bryan, Cazier, Sen and Young.

March 8th—Monday—Had hoped to have had seen Mr. Heywood amongst us by this time and to have had our contemplated party this evening, being the return of my natal day and completion of my fortieth year. Our settlement had done well during the winter and now making what preparations they can for the spring. The probability for my keeping school is rather slim as my health seems to continue poorly. Mary Shumway has been proposed by Bro. Bradley to teach if my health will not permit. It has also been thought of my living in the school house until I get a house of my own, that is if I can teach the school. I feel so very uncomfortable with Mary Anne. So many men around the house all the time and my health so poor. The baby has been improving in health since he was three months. Bro. Morley and Bro. Billings and Benjamin Johnson were here a few nights ago at which time Bro. Morley gave me a blessing written by Benjamin.

March 18th, 1852—Thursday—Mr. Heywood has arrived as also Bro. Benjamin Johnson with other company making a house full and the ball coming off makes a stirring time with us. This party is given in respect to Mr. Heywood and consequently I have to interest myself in it. Mrs. Heywood sent down a large cake made expressly for the occasion, also mince pies, so with custard pies and fried cakes we will make out an entertainment.

March 24th—Wednesday—Mr. Heywood left yesterday having stayed but one short week and during his stay the house being full of company and with him my visiting all the time I feel much prostrated in strength and health. The falling of the womb effects me worse than any previous time. My walking a greater distance and exerting myself about the party has hurt me much so that I can hardly do the least thing for myself. Mr. H. would like me to teach school and wishes me if it is practicable to get a boarding place or board with Mary Anne, but I know not yet what I will be able to do. I made out to give him a lot of caps and feel in the spirit to make as many as I can.

April 3rd—Sunday—A letter from Benjamin to Mary Anne in answer to her asking him "if she should board me" was anything but satisfactory to my mind and made me aware that there was statements made to him that was not correct.[4] I have written to him but Joseph Towndrows professed to have lost my letter.[5] It has altogether the appearance of a dark plot to get me out of the house as no doubt I am much in the way of the man.

April 22nd—Wednesday—Mr. Heywood returned here bringing with him Sister Vary with the calculation of her going on with the company to Iron County but concluded to remain and make out her visit here till Mr. H. would return to the city.

Monday evening—April 27th—The exploring company consisting of the Presidency and leading officers of the Territory arrived here on their way to the South.[6] During the evening we had several

---

[4] Tensions between Mary Anne Johnson, wife of Benjamin, and Martha had been percolating for some time; however, the diarist did not reveal the cause.

[5] Towndrows was evidently a mail carrier.

[6] On April 22, 1852, Brigham Young's party left Salt Lake City to visit the southern settlements and several Indian tribes. They returned to the city

calls—Judge Snow, and Lady, Bro. Kimball and his wife Mary Anne, Bro. & Sister Bean, Bro. and Sister Nobles, besides brethren G. A. Smith, Major Barlow to supper.[7] I requested of Bro. K. to bless my little boy which he did and gave him a good blessing.

May 1st—Saturday—Mr. H. got up a ride to celebrate the first of May by paying a visit to Clover Creek,[8] taking a wagon load of ladies, young and old. Sisters Cazier, Bryan, Vary, Candace, Sonsin, Mary Anne and myself. We visited Sister Love's who treated us sumptously.[9] While returning we were overtaken with a storm of wind, hail, snow and rain and had the wagon cover reefed off and a bow broken with the violence of the wind.

May 2nd—Sunday—Had a meeting to regulate about the school and it was decided that school would commence forthwith engaging Candace Smith to teach at the rate of five dollars a week and board herself.

May 11th—Mr. H. and Sister Vary started for Sanpete.

Started for the City, Monday morning, May 24th with Mr. H. and Sister Vary. My health very miserable. Called at Summit Creek and had dinner and supper which consisted of a right good cup of tea, etc. served up by Harriet in first rate style. Stayed over night at Petit Neat to Bro. Pace's.[10] I suffered much pain during the night in consequence of hurting myself by pulling the wagon to rights

---

on May 21. According to William Clayton, the group camped at Nephi on April 26 and organized itself. The party included sixty-four men, three boys, eleven women, one girl, thirty wagons, sixty-seven horses, and twelve mules— an impressive entourage. Clayton offered a good description of the fledgling settlements: "There are several beautiful settlements on the road to this point, among which, perhaps, Springville may rank the first, and Nephi the second. At both of these places the spirit of energy and industry is almost without a parallel. All the houses look clean and neat, fences in good order, and everything shows that saints live there. The city of Nephi was commenced in September last. There are now 20 good houses, a splendid corral for cattle, and a good quantity of land under cultivation." See *Deseret News*, May 15, 1852.

[7] George Washington Bean was one of the colorful characters of Mormon history. During his mission to Las Vegas he kept one notebook for himself and an official record for the church. In 1852 he was a young man of twenty-one. Israel Barlow had been long in the church and was one of the first nurserymen in Davis County.

[8] Clover Creek was settled a few months after Nephi and later renamed Mona. See McCune, *History of Juab County*, p. 137.

[9] Sister Love was a wife of Andrew Love, a prominent member of the community at Clover Creek.

[10] James Pace had been a member of the Mormon Battalion and was an adopted son of John D. Lee. One of the first settlers on Peteetneet Creek (named for a local Indian chief of note), Pace was honored by having the town renamed Pacen for him. Subsequently the spelling was changed to Payson. See Huff, *Memories That Live*, pp. 434, 439.

to sleep in. Called to see Sister Frances at Hobble Creek in the forenoon and dined at Provo to Bro. Bean's. Stayed over night to Bro.
Mercer's at American Fork [11] and next night arrived about six
o'clock to Mr. H.'s house in the city. Found the family all well
with the exception of Alley having the whooping cough and in one
week after Ida and my baby commenced coughing.

Attended meeting two Thursdays and the last Sabbath in the
New Tabernacle which I admire very much.[12] It is so neat and
unique in its appearance and economical in accommodating so many.
I heard Bro. Brigham preach and was delighted with his remarks.

Have returned from the city after spending about three weeks
there, not as pleasant as I could have wished which I attribute in a
great measure to my health being miserable and all the children
have the whooping cough, but feel considerably better after my
journey homeward. Truly I feel this little settlement my home altho
I have no house as yet nor the first appearance of one but the place
and people are near and dear to me. I enjoyed the ride more particularly as I had much conversation with Mr. H. which I have been
deprived of since the time he came down accompanied by Sister
Vary, tho in company ever since I have not felt the least freedom in
communicating a thought to him and that for the space of two
months.

We have now commenced boarding with Sister Bryan who
seems to be the right kind of person to live with and Bro. Bryan[13]
is so sensible and social that their house seems a little paradise to me,
to what and where I have lived. Our garden has been some injured
by the flowing over of the water from Bro. Johnson's and my flower
and other seeds have been nearly all destroyed. There is not the first
thing done towards the house.

To our great surprise we found that Candace left for Manti
vacating her situation after six weeks of trial of it; she being some
what dissatisfied with some of the people and the people generally
dissatisfied with her management as School Teacher. And as I
formed an opinion of her inefficiency as a teacher I expected sooner
or later she would have to resign. But I was disappointed in her not

[11] The 1850 Census lists a John Mercer in Utah County.

[12] Martha was referring, of course, to what is presently known as the Old
Tabernacle (demolished). Built of adobe on the southwest corner of Temple
Square, the first tabernacle was 126 feet long, 64 feet wide, and could seat
twenty-five hundred. The ground is now occupied by the Assembly Hall. The
tabernacle had been dedicated on April 6, 1852. See Jenson, *Church Chronology*,
p. 45.

[13] Probably Charles H. Bryan, a Nephi alderman.

showing more interest in the welfare of the school and keeping her time, two things she was very remiss in—.

Mary Anne Johnson does not return to this place at present.

July 12, 1852—Monday—Commenced school this day with 17 scholars. My health being some better than it has for a long time [,] realizing that my getting better health and also having a girl to help me with the baby [, I have been] spending my time during the two weeks that Mr. H. has been gone in my garden.

Attended Sabbath School yesterday and was surprised that there was no teacher there, it being the 2nd Sabbath of my attendance finding no one there with the exception of Bro. Baxter who is the superintendent. We have now commenced our Sabbath School at eight o'clock in the morning, being the same time that they hold [it] in Great Salt Lake City. There was some difficulty in the people to agree about having a daily school. The trustees had a meeting two Sundays ago being the Sunday before Mr. H. left and Bro. Foote was not for having the school started until it was ascertained how many families would send. He also volunteered to go round to ascertain this point and report the next Sunday afternoon at which time they decided on meeting. I was proposed as teacher until a suitable one could be obtained.

The next Sabbath it was reported that some of the brethren objected to the salary of five dollars a week for the teacher and would not send. The foremost of such were Amos Gustin, Elmore and Miller.[14] Bryan having an opportunity [of] offering his mind to Gustin & Miller, they confessed they were wrong and Gustin said it was Bro. Foote drew it out of him and Miller's excuse was because Gustin and Elmore objected he did.

Brother Bradley [15] having returned from the city Saturday, he called a meeting yesterday and proposed that those who desired a school would subscribe so much each as they felt would be wisdom. This plan took at once, Bro. Foote being absent. Bro. Bryan took out his pencil and amongst those present there was over seventy dollars collected.

July 19th, 1852—Sunday—Attended Sabbath school this morning and found the superintendent, Bro. Baxter present who acted as teacher with myself, making two teachers and fourteen scholars. My

[14] Amos Gustin and Josiah Miller were early Nephi settlers. Elmore has not been identified.

[15] Probably George Bradley.

school during the week was as interesting as I could expect considering the great deficiency of the children.

Had two letters by last week's mail, one from Mr. H. and one from Bro. Rose,[16] also a note from Mrs. H. They are all sick from influenza colds in the city which reminds me the more how much health I have gained since I left the city and my baby now recovering from the whooping cough; his teeth have caused him some indisposition and considering it with the whooping cough I consider he is doing right well. He is very small for his age; now so thin but so much better than Ida and Alley.

July 25th—Sunday—Attended Sabbath School this morning with Bro. Baxter, making two teachers. We had 16 scholars. Had a letter from my husband informing me of his expecting to be with us very soon—he will probably leave the city today.

My health has been very poorly today probably on account of over working yesterday on Bro. Rose's muffs and partly by taking cold. The baby is also miserable. The weather has been very warm yesterday and today which prostrates me much. We were agreeably surprised by Bro. Jones [17] from Sanpete coming among [us] and preaching for us and so glad was I to have an opportunity of hearing him that I went to hear him but I had to return before it was out.

August 1st—Sunday—Was disappointed during the last week in Mr. H. not coming down. Heard that he was detained by court business and the election. I have had Sister Davis to work for me during last week and the Saturday previous. Next Thursday she expects to go to Provo to recover her cows and oxen that her cidevant husband stole from her.

My baby is recovering from the whooping cough but is some troubled with teething. He is now eight months and a half and none through yet. My health is mending gradually and thus far I have been able to keep the school without any serious inconvenience. The number rose to twenty one day. Friday forenoon had but eight scholars and did not keep in the afternoon for that reason. I continue to enjoy boarding with Sister Bryan very much.

August 16—Monday—Resume school today after a week's absence on account of Mr. and Mrs. Heywood's being here with the

[16] This may have been Ralph Rose of Canada who is listed in the 1850 Census.

[17] Probably Dan Jones.

children and Mary Bell,[18] who all returned to the city last Thursday morning. We had a very pleasant time while they were here with the exception of Sister Heywood having the toothache pretty severe the last day and night. I received a letter from Mrs. Strong and one from Mrs. Leamond in the city.

Was not able to attend meeting or Sabbath School yesterday on account of my baby being sick. He has the canker together with his teething,—seems to keep him down very much. My own and Sister Bryan's health is but poorly since our visitors left. Bro. Johnson has been here with his wife Harriet and has decided on bringing his oldish wife and her children to come here instead of Mary Anne.

August 30—Monday—Resumed school today after a week's absence on account of ill health. Heard from Mr. H. on Saturday who has been ill since his return to the city. Mailed two letters last week for Rochester to Mr. Hayes and Mrs. Strong. Sent 16 caps to the city and also 14 the week before.[19] Yesterday spent the day to Clover Creek. Took the ride with the object of receiving benefit to my health. Had a pleasant time with the folks there—visited with Bro. and Sister Bigelow as also with Brethren Love and Wolf and Sisting.[20]

September 19—Sunday—Mr. Heywood came here on Friday, 10th inst., at which time Major Wells and Company was here to attend to the Military exercises of the brethren of this place.[21] Brethren Wells, Robinson and ladies spent part of the day with us. This last week the flooring has been laid in the school-house and hearth set and tomorrow I again resume my school. My own and my baby's health being but poorly I suffer much in trying to teach school but being Mr. H.'s wish to do so I make the attempt.

---

[18] Mary Bell, Heywood's fourth wife, was born in 1839 in Scotland. Heywood was twenty-four years her senior. However, it seems likely that the couple did not marry until Mary Bell reached her fifteenth year, as family genealogical charts show Mary receiving her endowments on March 31, 1854.

[19] To make a total of thirty caps in addition to all her other duties seems a great task. Heywood evidently had a regular outlet for them. Later, they made their own sales station.

[20] Martha was visiting the families of Andrew Love, James O. Bigelow, and John A. Wolfe at Mona (Clover Creek). Brother Sisting has not been identified. See McCune, *History of Juab County*, p. 137.

[21] Daniel Hanmer Wells was elected major-general of the Nauvoo Legion on May 26, 1849. On March 27, 1852, he received the rank of lieutenant-general but was not commissioned by Brigham Young until March 7, 1855. See Jenson, *LDS Biographical Encyclopedia*, 1:62–63. Despite military exercises and the building of forts, some settlements had to be abandoned during the Walker War.

September 28th—Tuesday—On last Saturday, being the 25th, we celebrated the anniversary of our settling this place. We met in the school house at about eleven o'clock with our invited guests, Father Morley and lady with several others from San Pete and Bro. Benjamin Johnson and their ladies from Summit Creek. The Clover Creek folks were invited but did not come with the exception of Sister Bigelow. We had also new settlers who arrived the night before, Bros. Udell and Vickers (English), also brethren from Iron County on their way to the city. We had excellent remarks from Father Morley who referred to his past experiences—also from Bro. Johnson who also referred to his past experiences in the Church. The most of the company then adjourned while the tables were set and at about three o'clock we took our seats. Our feast was composed of what we had raised in our settlement during the last year and made a very handsome appearance—chickens cooked in various ways, vegetables, preserves made with water melon molasses, cake, bread of flour raised here, wine of choke-cherries and we found that our house was far too small to accommodate the people.

October 1st—Friday—Mr. Heywood left us this morning for the city. Same day Capt. Sherwood's company of 17 wagons arrived on their way to San Bernardino.[22] This afternoon completes two weeks since the floor was laid that I have kept school.

October 17th—Saturday—Today we were agreeably surprised with a visit from Bro. Parley Pratt and two of his wives on their way to the city from his mission. He preached on the subject of his mission and the peculiar providence that opened to him to defray not only the same but to liberate him from debt contracted previous to his departure from Gr. S. L. City, as also the manners and customs of the Chileans in South America where he sojourned for a season in which place his wife Phebe gave birth to child and lost it at two months old. I was not able to attend but the first part of the evening on account of the irritability of my baby.

I was again obliged to adjourn school last Wednesday noon on account of poor health. Just completed weaning my baby and find him some better by so doing but my own health is miserable.

[22] This may have been Henry G. Sherwood, first city marshal of Nauvoo, who helped settle and survey the new Mormon community at San Bernardino, California. Later he apostatized. See Leonard J. Arrington, *Charles C. Rich: Mormon General and Western Frontiersman* (Provo, Ut.: Brigham Young University Press, 1974), pp. 189–90.

George A. Smith preached here at which time Bro. Jacob Bigler [23] arrived here. The brethren are arriving fast in this place now.

October 24—Sunday—Yesterday the brethren who are going on their several missions southward commenced coming to this place and this evening the last came in. There are about twenty in number, several of whom I had some little acquaintance with and some just got acquainted with. N.V. Jones, Bishop of the 15th Ward on his way to Calcutta, formerly of Rochester, who I had long desired to become acquainted with, of which I failed to affect till now on his journey to other lands. I had a very pleasant visit with him, as also with Brothers Woolley and Ballantyne. Three meetings, last evening and today fore and after noon. [24]

October 31—Sunday—Mr. Heywood returned here about ten o'clock last night after we had retired to bed and Judge Snow a few hours previous, who preached for us on the subject of education, schools and school houses and I enjoyed his remarks much. This evening I had a very agreeable visit with him while the brethren were engaged in a business meeting.

Monday morning accompanied Mr. H. and Judge Snow to San Pete, arrived at Father Morley's about 4 o'clock in the evening. Found Sister Theresa Kimball laid up with rheumatism. Was very sick that night myself. Next day was not able to go out anywhere but enjoyed myself well in Father Morley's family, considering my own and baby's sickness. I like the appearance of San Pete better than I supposed I would. Left the next morning and returned here about 4 o'clock. The weather was intensely cold, on which night, being the 3rd of November, we had a very severe frost which injured most vegetation; coming so unexpected the brethren were not fully prepared for it.

[23] Jacob G. Bigler, early Nephi settler and later first president of Juab Stake.

[24] A special conference of elders was convened on August 28, 1852, in Salt Lake City. A hundred missionaries were called to various foreign fields, and the following day the first public proclamation of celestial (plural) marriage was made. Nathaniel V. Jones, Samuel A. Woolley, and Richard Ballantyne were among those sent to "Hindoostan." See *Deseret News,* September 18, 1852. Jones had been a member of the Mormon Battalion and was to serve as president of the mission to India. He helped develop the territory's fledgling iron industry. Woolley, a brother of Edwin D., was among the first settlers at Parowan and later was bishop of the Salt Lake City Ninth Ward. Ballantyne had a varied career as an Ogden merchant, farmer, and railroad builder. He founded the LDS Sunday School system. After returning from India, he lived in Nephi for two years before the Utah War. For more information on these three men see Jenson, *LDS Biographical Encyclopedia,* 2:368–69, 1:781–82, 1:703–6.

November 11th—Thursday evening Brother Ezra T. Benson
and S.M. Blair, arrived here on their return from the city and
preached for us.[25] I could not attend on account of my baby but
heard of his preaching which was excellent. They started the next
morning after expressing their desire to Mr. H. to have lots each
set down to them. We have now 44 families residing in this place,
the majority of which are very, very desirable citizens.

The bridge on the Sevier has been completed by our brethren
in this place under the supervision of Bro. Foote, he having got the
contract from Bro. Young, as also the bridge over Chicken Creek.[26]
The Fort has had quite a start, having four rooms reared of adobes,
two belonging to us, one which we will occupy, the other rent to
Bro. Bently and two rooms for a tithing house to be occupied by
Bishop Bigler, who is our Presiding Bishop. I feel well satisfied to
neighbor with those two families. As for Sister Bentley I consider
it a providential circumstance to have her so near me. May the Lord
bless our acquaintance and should we become friends, indeed, may
it be in the Lord.

Mr. H.'s health has been very poorly during the last week
which we lay to the weather. Joseph Neal, my baby, has been
gaining since our return from San Pete. His diarrhea has ceased
with the canker. My health is rather better but not very well at that.
I have some reason to expect that I am about five months in a
state of pregnancy but my symptoms and feelings are so different
from what I had with my boy that I sometimes am inclined to doubt
that such is my case.

November 15th—Monday—Last Friday there was the body of
a man found in the forks of the creek having the appearance of
being shot in the forehead, covered with two coats. The discovery
was made by Bro. Cumming's youngest son. Next day another body
was found a few rods westward of the former having the appearance

[25] Benson, an LDS apostle, served many church missions and was a ter-
ritorial official. See Jenson, *LDS Biographical Encyclopedia*, 1:99–102. Seth M.
Blair, a lawyer, was U. S. district attorney. In 1859 he, James Ferguson, and
Hosea Stout published the *Mountaineer*, a periodical denouncing the rule of
federal judges in Utah. See Roberts, *Comprehensive History*, 4:522. Benson and
Blair had left Salt Lake City on November 2. Benson reported in the *Deseret
News* of November 27, 1852, that Nephi had "26 families of the Fall emigration"
and was beginning "to extend her borders and assume quite a village ap-
pearance."

[26] Benson's letter, cited above, praised the Sevier bridge and said "much
credit was due bro. Foot."

of being shot in the back of the neck. Both bodies had United States Livery on them.[27]

November 28th—Sunday—Mr. Heywood left here last Thursday the 25th in company with Bros. Fox and Eldrige. The snow on the ground is about two feet high. We here had the greatest snowstorm I have experienced in the Valley. It commenced last Monday night, 22nd, and continued all day Tuesday and during the night but ceased gradually after daylight. It has been thawing ever since and has now commenced raining, giving every appearance of the snow going off.

A week ago last Thursday my little boy attained to the completion of the first year of his life for which I thank my Heavenly Father and have faith that His heavenly mercy will continually protect his infant years and baffle his predisposition to disease.

Brethren Erastus Snow and Franklin Richards arrived here on their way to Parowan on Tuesday the 15th and preached here the same night.[28]

December 1st.—Wednesday night took possession of my room yesterday and commenced housekeeping today. The snow has been going off considerably but the weather continues unsettled and more or less stormy.

December 5th—Sunday—Still continues unsettled. Snowed some today and last evening. It thundered and lightened and a smart shower of rain.

December 12th, 1852—Sunday—The weather has turned cold and clear the last 36 hours but little work has been done in this place the last month or six weeks, but it looks now as if we were going to have settled cold weather. My cow calved yesterday afternoon which proves indeed a blessing to me at this time. I begin to feel tolerably comfortable in my little home.

---

[27] The *Deseret News* of December 11, 1852, contains a letter dated November 13, 1852, from J. L. Heywood in Nephi, describing the finding of the two bodies and their appearance. An inquest was being held on the first victim when the second body was discovered. The *News* requested other newspapers to publish the murders in the hope of identifying the victims. Heywood, as U. S. marshal, was officially interested in the crime. The Cummings who discovered the first body is unknown. A Benjamin F. Cummings is listed in the 1850 Census in Weber.

[28] Snow and Richards had left Salt Lake City on November 11, 1852, with a company of ironmongers for the southern settlements. See Snow's letter in the *Deseret News* of December 25, 1852.

We had the first dance for this season on Friday night as a reward for getting the school house repaired. School commenced last Wednesday—Brother Spencer teacher.

Thursday evening Brethren Snow and Richards and also Father Morley preached in the school house on their way to the city. My baby's health continues to improve and my own health is tolerably good. Enjoy keeping house right well.

January 2nd, 1853—Sunday—Last Tuesday evening the brethren had a meeting for the purpose of taking into consideration what it was best to do in regard to the cattle during the inclemency of the weather, having lost seven head the day before in consequence of the storm on Sunday, making 11 head of cattle and two calves within the last month. It was decided that there would be a united effort of prayer to our Heavenly Father to mittigate the severity of the weather by giving us a thaw and that a certain number of the oxen be kept up to procure firewood, and the milk cows, etc. The brethren on their return home after the meeting gave the notice as extensively as they could and the first thing I realized on awaking the next morning was a thorough thaw which continued steady ever since, so that we have prospect now of our cattle doing well and the roads to Mill becoming passable. My little Neal is improving steadily day by day and is much changed in appearance for the last month—is very lovely and interesting.

Yesterday being New Year's day Brother Foote gave the hands that worked on the bridge a supper and dance. I had a special invitation from Sister Foote which extended to Sister Candace Smith who is staying with me.[29] And I must say, a better party I have not attended in the Valley, nor up to this time have we had so good a one in this place. It will be remembered long in this place to Bro. Foote's credit. There was a picnic party to School house on Christmas day and a wedding party to Amos Gustin's house.

January 9th—Sunday—Had rather poor health during the last week. Last Sunday attended meeting and in so doing took fresh cold and on Thursday morning had a very severe spell of bowel complaint which prostrated me very much till today. Feeling somewhat better and was able to go and settle up a grievance that I caused by joking spirit towards Sister Weldon who is staying at Bro. Brad-

[29] Candace lived in Manti with Albert and Esther Smith. She was about nineteen years old at this time. She was one of several young women who stayed with Martha from time to time to help with the household chores.

ley's. She did not seem very willing to forgive—she went through the form but manifested a hard spirit towards me afterward.

We had rather pleasant weather last week—thawed some and snowed some but rather gained on the thawing. Have not heard from Mr. Heywood tho the mail came in last week and brought papers.[30] My baby still gains in health and strength.

January 16th—Sunday—Candace left this place for San Pete last Wednesday having been staying with me for about five weeks. I realized her departure quite a pleasant circumstance. We had a very pleasant afternoon visit to Sister Foote's the day previous terminating with the dancing school which I enjoyed very well, the only one I attended.

February 6th—Sunday—Mr. Heywood returned here last Tuesday, first of the month in good health, in company with Father Morley and Petit of San Pete. On Wednesday we had a Partriarchal Blessing meeting all day and continued next day. A very good spirit prevailed during Father Morley's stay. From the time Candace left till Mr. H. came I seemed to be gaining in health and strength but of late have felt some what slimmer owing to overdoing a little and taking cold.

February 20, 1853—Sunday—Snow pretty solid yet on the ground up to this date. We have had two or three days of warm sun as yet but the weather has been clear tho cold for the last two weeks, freezing very hard at night. No travelling across the divide to Sanpete as yet. Bro. Boswell just returned by the south route.

We have had good meetings in this place and a good spirit seems to prevail among the people generally. Mr. Heywood has given two historical lectures that have been well received and proposes to get up a literary society which I think will go.[31] Brother Spencer as a teacher is generally liked.[32] Yesterday had a meeting

---

[30] According to a notice in the *Deseret News* of December 8, 1853, the southern mail for Manti and the towns in between left Salt Lake City Mondays at 6 A.M. and returned Saturdays at 6 P.M.

[31] A letter of Samuel Pitchforth in Nephi to Joseph Cain, dated March 1, 1853, and published in the *Deseret News* of March 19, 1853, described the settlement and the activities there very well. He commented on a dancing school and a cyphering school, the unity of the Saints, the work being done by Walker's Indians, and the crops. He said that Heywood had been lecturing on the history and geography of those countries to which elders had been recently sent. Pitchforth indicated that the people had received these talks so well that Heywood was encouraged to start a literary association and to propose that "members subscribe towards a library." A bit boastful of these activities, Pitchforth added, "you can see that our president don't intend Nephi to be far in the rear."

[32] Probably George Spencer. See McCune, *History of Juab County*, p. 76.

for the Indians who had been baptized last summer and the old captain whose name is Pooro ———— was ordained and made known some interesting facts to the brethren by means of Bro. Hold [?] who is the interpreter concerning his faith and doctrine.[33]

Today our meeting was much disturbed by Batiste[?][34] who came in seemingly possessed with a bad spirit. He was in a very great passion and charged our brethren with having written to Brigham to have him killed and charged Bro. Elmore with having threatened killing some of his men and then they asked for something to eat.

March 6th—Sunday—Sister Mary Anne Johnson arrived here from Summit Creek a week ago last Friday—February 25th—on a visit, her health not very good and expects to be confined in a few [?] and her opportunity to return is uncertain as the travelling is bad just at this time.

Mr. H.'s health has been but poorly for the last two weeks as likewise my own. It is all that I can do to attend to the house work that is necessary without attempting any sewing work. The Spring weather is advancing rapidly, the snow is wearing away very fast yet still there is a great body of it on the ground.

There was organized on last evening a society called The Mount Nebo Literary Association — President, Treasurer, Secretary and twelve directors.

The California mail passed through on Friday the 4th and stayed over night, bringing the news of General Pearce being elected President of the United States.[35]

---

[33] The Indian and the interpreter have not been identified.

[34] Possibly "Old Battiste" or "Battest" mentioned in Peter Gottfredson, *Indian Depredations in Utah* (Salt Lake City, 1919), pp. 21, 102.

[35] Franklin Pierce, the fourteenth president, had served as colonel and then brigadier-general in the Mexican War. Pierce, a dark-horse candidate, received the Democratic nomination on the forty-ninth ballot. He went on to sweep the election in November 1852 from Gen. Winfield Scott, another Mexican War figure. Since national news came to Utah via California during the winter season, the southern settlements were aware of important events a day or two before the leaders in Salt Lake City.

*March 20th—Sunday—*Mr. Heywood left here last Thursday, 17th, having been with us full six weeks. The Sabbath previous to his leaving—13 inst.—held a conference for the purpose of taking a vote in reference to the officers of this place. Brothers Sly [1] and Foote voted against Mr. H. and Brother Bradley [2] and a few did not vote either way. Otherwise the voting for all the officers was unanimous. Bro. Sly's remarks were so much out of place and manifesting an opposition spirit to Mr. Heywood that it was voted and carried that he should be cut off from the church. The day before Mr. H. left here Bro. Foote called on him for the purpose of settling the matter with him and proposing to do better for the future. Mr. H. gave him to understand that he would not be satisfied without making the plaster as large as the wound which meant that he must make a public confession before and also make acknowledgements to Bros. Bradley and Bigler.

*March 27th—Sunday—*Attended meeting where Bro. Foote made his public acknowledgement in regard to conduct to Bro. Heywood but did not include or refer to Brethren Bradley and Bigler.

[1] This may have been James Calvin Sly, a member of the Mormon Battalion, who evidently lived in Juab County. He died at Chicken Creek in 1864. See Jenson, *LDS Biographical Encyclopedia,* 3:514.

[2] George W. Bradley directed the Juab militia and built a grist mill. See McCune, *History of Juab County,* pp. 56, 73, 90.

Bro. Sly on being asked if he wished to make any remarks attempted a confession which had more the spirit of justification of his course than contrition and was not accepted. I noticed that Brethren Bradley and Miller [3] had much power in their remarks.

We had quite a severe snowstorm last Thursday but since then the weather has been fair but rather cold. The delinquency of the mail is truly vexatious. Last week came so far as Springville and returned altho there has been quite a number of wagons bound for California along during the last week.

April 3rd—Sunday—Spring now appears. Had no storm during the last week but yet the air is cold. Spring work has hardly commenced in this place. Quite a number of our folks are now on their way to Conference. Had a letter from Mr. H. last Wednesday which intimated that his and all the rest of the family's health was good. Nealy started to walk on his own accord last Monday and has progressed well since. Is cutting his eye teeth at present; his health is right good. Attended meeting which was well attended considering the absence of so many.

April 24th—Sunday—Left this place for the city on Wednesday morning the 6th to attend conference by message from Mr. Heywood given me by mail driver. Arrived at Provo that night and put up to Bro. G. A. Smith's and found his wife Lucy there rather indisposed—had a good visit with her. Next day drove to Willow Creek and stayed over night to Gernsy Brown's.[4] His wife with whom I was well acquainted when Harriet Young, was from home which was some disappointment to me but I was much pleased to find her possessed of so good a home. Next day arrived in the city about noon and found all the folks in good health. Attended meeting that afternoon and heard Elder John Taylor preach. His text was— "As it was in the beginning, etc." I was interested in his remarks but felt very tired and oppressed before meeting was closed.

On leaving the Tabernacle Mr. H. proposed calling on Sister Hyde [5] to which I gladly assented and enjoyed the interview so well that with the previous fatigue of sitting in meeting and the travelling prostrated me to that degree that I suffered all the time I remained there.

[3] Josiah Miller, one of the first Nephi settlers, was to be elected mayor of the town in May 1852. Miles Miller was a town councilor. Ibid., pp. 56, 61.

[4] Gurnsey Brown and many other Browns were settlers at Willow Creek (Draper). See Kirkham and Lundstrom, *Tales of a Triumphant People*, p. 229.

[5] Probably a wife of Apostle Orson Hyde.

Started from the city on Monday morning 18th for home by mail, as also Mr. H. with his own team taking Bro. and Sister Barber [6] with all their appertenances to move them to Nephi, and supposing it would be so much more comfortable for me to travel by mail, I started according, but found out our mistake before night. We stopped at Dry Creek that night with Sister Barber's brother and were well entertained.[7] Next day we traveled to Provo by noon and had good refreshments to Bro. Bean's and from thence by evening to Springville where we had the best kind of accommodations to Bro. Humphrey's.[8] Dined next day to Bro. Shumway's [9] Petit Neat and expected to have stayed to Bro. Johnson's but Mary Anne was just taken in labor and we have learned since that the result was a fine boy. (Mr. H. had a letter from Benjamin which he has answered and I added a few lines.) This circumstance prevented us from stopping there so we made for Clover Creek and put up to Bro. Bigelow's and found ourselves home by noon next day. Amelia Fellows who came to live with me two days before I started for the city did as well in charge of my affairs as I could expect.[10]

May 8th—Sunday—The Presidential company arrived here on Monday afternoon, April 25th about three o'clock.[11] We had the pleasure of entertaining to supper, Bro. Brigham Young and wife Margaret,[12] Bro. Heber Kimball and wife Vilate, Bro. John Taylor and wife Leonora [13] and Judge Snow. Many of the brethren called. Sister Vilate stayed over night and nearly all who supped breakfasted with us. They left here for Manti about 9 o'clock and returned

[6] This may have been Luke and Susan Barber who are listed in the 1850 Census in Salt Lake City.

[7] Dry Creek was renamed Lehi.

[8] Smith Humphrey is listed in the 1850 Census in Utah County.

[9] Charles Shumway and his son Andrew were pioneers of 1847 and early settlers at Manti. They may have had interests in the Payson area as well.

[10] Amelia Fellows, listed as age thirteen in the 1850 Census, would seem to have been another of the young girls whom Martha found more troublesome than helpful to have in her household.

[11] Brigham Young and his party left Salt Lake City April 20, 1853, to visit Indians in the southern settlements, partly as a result of information from Iron County that seemed to portend trouble from Indians. At Provo on April 23, Young in his dual role as governor and superintendent of Indian affairs issued a proclamation accusing "a horde of Mexicans, or outlandish men," of stirring up the Indians and selling them arms and ammunition contrary to territorial and federal law. Officers of the territory were to place the Mexicans in "safe custody." See *Deseret News,* April 30, 1853.

[12] Margaret Pierce. Another wife of that first name, Margaret Maria Alley, had died the previous year.

[13] Leonora Cannon was Taylor's first wife and a sister of George Cannon, father of George Q. Cannon.

from there on Friday evening the 30th. We had a change of company. Those that we had before went to Bishop Bigler's and in return we were honored with Bro. G. A. and wife Bathsheba,[14] Sister Amanda Kimball, Brethren Hunter, Blair, Ezra T. Benson, etc. Sister Vilate would stay with [us] in spite of counsel about the same company breakfasting in the morning. They all seemed to enjoy themselves remarkably well and none more than Bro. Brigham. They started from here about 9 o'clock Saturday morning for the city. I had a delightful visit with Sisters Taylor and Kimball the first evening. It would seem as if the President's life was somewhat in danger by a peculiar circumstance happening to him on his way from the city.[15]

Today (the 8th) attended forenoon meeting during which time Brother Lewis Robinson with a Brother Whalock [?] arrived in our settlement on his way to hunt up some horse thieves, one of which had wintered in this place, boarding with Father Gifford, named Llingerline.[16] Quite a number of our folks were baptized today and confirmed. Last Sabbath Mr. H. was baptized for his health, also Bro. Sly who was cut off the Church about two months ago. Mr. H. went to San Pete last Monday morning and returned on Thursday night. The trip helped his health some. Weather is rather dry for this time of the year and also rather cold. Considerable ploughing and seeding has been done and is going on briskly.

Last week's Deseret [News] brought news from the eastern papers regarding Orson Pratt's movements in Washington.[17] Their

---

[14] Bathsheba W. Bigler was George A. Smith's first wife.

[15] While at Provo the president was accosted by an unknown man who carried arms on his person. The stranger said he had "400 Mexicans awaiting my orders" and as many more as he wanted plus Indians. This circumstance apparently led to Young's issuance of a proclamation that called for Mexicans to be put in "safe custody." Young described his southern journey at a meeting in the tabernacle May 8; his address was published in the *Deseret News* of May 14, 1853.

[16] Robinson's traveling companion was probably Cyrus H. Wheelock, a gifted orator who later became president of the Northern States Mission of the LDS church. See Jenson, *LDS Biographical Encyclopedia*, 4:363. When complaints of horse thieves reached the ears of Brigham Young, the sage leader said he seldom lost any of his possessions because he watched them or set others to watch them. See *Deseret News*, May 14, 1853. Nothing is known of accused horse thieves Llingerline or Vaughan who is mentioned in the next entry.

[17] Apostle Orson Pratt had been sent to Washington in 1852 to take charge of all the branches of the LDS church east of the Rocky Mountains, including those in the British provinces. There he published *The Seer*, the first issues of which devoted themselves to the defense of celestial marriage. See Thomas Edgar Lyon, "Orson Pratt—Early Mormon Leader" (M.A. thesis, University of Chicago, 1932), pp. 62–64.

opinion amounts to this, that it is best to let us as a people alone and we will soon become extinct.

May 15th—Sunday—On Tuesday evening the mail came in and brought me two very agreeable letters, one from my brother and the other from my old friend Mrs. Hayes in Rochester. By the same mail Mr. Heywood had news from the city concerning court matters that first took him to San Pete and then to the city very unexpectedly. Next morning by daylight Bro. Hoyt (who is marshall) called on Mr. H. to let him know that one of the horse thieves, Vaughan, was in the place. Orders for his capture were immediately given. Mr. H. return[ed] from San Pete on Thursday evening and started by mail on Friday morning for the city.

May 27th—Friday—May 27th Mr. H. in company with Bro. Hiram Kimball arrived here very unexpectedly.[18] Mr. H. after his horses and wheat and the latter after tithing wheat. They came by the new route on the west side of the Jordan in accordance with Bro. Brigham's request. They found the road much better than might be anticipated but yet rough enough to require some labor to make it tolerable. They returned the same way the next day at noon with their teams and a number of our brethren started with them to escort them about twenty miles to make the road some better. One great advantage of this new road will be in time of high water and also when there is considerable snow on the old route.

June 5th—Sabbath—I was startled with the intelligence of the death of Mr. H.'s little girl and continued some days not knowing the particulars, not even which child. Since then I have had a letter from Mr. H. giving them, 48 hours before she died (Alice Grafton) she complained of a pain in her head and the morning of the day she died she was dressing by her mother who did not perceive anything very alarming in her symptoms till about 11 o'clock when she was taken with spasms and at five in the afternoon died.[19] The endearing and remarkably interesting little Ally, the love of all who knew her; being about the hour that her father and his friend Hiram Kimball sat down to supper in this house, being Friday the 27th day of May. The grief of the family in the City must be intense and her poor mother consequently the most stricken. Oh, that she may be blessed and preserved in this her hour of affliction, and that

[18] Hiram S. Kimball, a son of Phineas and Abigail, was a pioneer of 1850.

[19] Alice Grafton (Ally) Heywood died on May 27, 1853, at age five years and six months. Eliza R. Snow wrote a memorial poem on the sad occasion. See *Deseret News*, June 18, 1853.

we all as a family may be profited thereby. My health is but poorly and I realize that this stroke of affliction affects me and as I again draw nearer to the period of again becoming a mother I feel more weakly and quite unable to perform any labor. My sweet little boy seems to gain day by day in health and strength for which I bless thee, my heavely father, as long as he lives he will be the living likeness of his dear sister Alice who loved him very very much. But she is now gone to the spirit world to see, be with and make acquaintance with infant brother, the first born of the children.[20]

June 8th—Wednesday—Sister Melissa Johnson who lost her babe in the winter and Sister Harriet with her babe, a very large fine boy 5 months old, took a ride and stayed over night.

Received a letter from Mr. H. bearing date of June 14th, referring to the high water of City Creek doing great damage to property in the city [21] and also at Provo where three persons have been drowned during the past week and also of the conviction of Wm. May for the murder of Gochu [?].[22] The testimony of Joseph Towndrow was the principal evidence of his guilt.

July 15th, 1853—Mr. and Mrs. Heywood arrived here about 1 o'clock Friday night accompanied by Bro. Johnson and Archy Bell and without any protections. Monday evening following Bros. George A. Smith and Stewart arrived with a guard bringing intelligence of a man on guard being shot at Petit Neat.[23] Brother Stewart the next day realized the loss of a very fine span of horses, put into Bro. Foote's stable and taken away during the night with a horse belonging to one of our brethren here.

January 1st, 1854—Mr. Heywood left here for the city Monday morning, November 28th in his own team, Brother George and his wife going up to the city with him and by his leaving and George having a house built for himself I got possession of our other room for the first time. Mr. H. told me on leaving that I might make what improvements I had a mind to and he would realter what did

[20] Evidently Sarepta's first child, a boy, had died as an infant.

[21] Heavy runoffs did considerable damage in Salt Lake City, especially in Heywood's Seventeenth Ward where City Creek cut a deep channel and threatened homes. See Jenson, *Church Chronology*, p. 84.

[22] William May was convicted of first degree murder on June 8, 1853, and sentenced to be executed on January 13, 1854. The day before the sentence was to have been carried out, Brigham Young issued a reprieve. See Utah Territory, Executive Papers, 1850–55, Utah State Archives, State Capitol, Salt Lake City.

[23] Alexander Keel was killed July 18, 1853.

not suit him when he returned. The first thing I had done was the doorway made between the rooms and a window place put on the east end, the floors refilled and nailed down; and when I accomplished all this I had a family of the name of Bennett to come in and enjoy the fruits of my labor.

My little daughter was born August 8th, a very healthy child. Mr. H. was not here at the time but arrived two days after her birth. I did not suffer quite so much as I did with my boy. From taking cold in changing me 24 hours after her birth I had quite an ill turn the third night and it might have proved serious if it had not been for the unwearied attention of Sister Gifford. And another great advantage I devised was having my breasts drawn by a little girl named Josephine Sperry. We named our little one Sarepta Maria after Mrs. Heywood and my mother. She had the honor of being born in the midst of Indian difficulties, when there were express running all over the country and martial law pervading in all the settlements.[24] Mr. H. again left me when she was about three weeks old. I felt very bad the morning he left me; it seemed I could not bear to be left alone and also what might happen to him on the way.

The Saturday after he left the San Pete brethren arrived here on their way to the city to attend conference and brought with them the bodies of three murdered brethren, by the Indians, out of four who started from the San Pete the day before the company did. They had not obeyed counsel in camping where they did that night. They were very much mutilated and the other one was found and brought in the next day.

This barbarous circumstance actuated our brethren, counselled by Father Morley of San Pete (who no doubt was much excited in the time of it) and President Call of Filmore, to do quite as barbarous an act the following morning, being the Sabbath. Nine Indians coming into our Camp looking for protection and bread with us, because we promised it to them and without knowing they did the first evil act in that affair or any other, were shot down without one minute's notice. I felt satisfied in my own mind that if Mr. Heywood had been here they would not have been dealt with so unhumanly. It cast considerable gloom over my mind. Mr. H. has told me on leaving to do all I could to encourage them by employing them to work for me.[25]

[24] The Walker War had erupted in July 1853.

[25] This incident of the Walker War is told in different terms by Gottfredson in *Indian Depredations,* pp. 74–75. According to that work, William Luke,

April 9th, 1854—Sunday—My little girl was eight months old yesterday and from the time of her birth she has been very healthy indeed. I have been to the city and spent four weeks there and one week in travelling there and returning making just five weeks from home and while there Mr. H. was here in company with Bros. Pack and Fosgreen. I left the house and concerns with Bro. and Sister Broadhead who took good care of everything in my house.

Reflections—The winter has passed and brought and left its several changes. Our settlement has undergone many changes. One year ago three families stood here on the fort ground and right in sight westward was Bro. Foote's good two story adobe house and about 40 houses scatter around. And now we are all brought together on this very same fort ground to the amount of about 125 houses, or at least that number of families.[26]

Indian hostilities seem to be suspended for the present and ploughing and seeding time is the present excitement amongst our people but there is considerable of a change with the Indians. They appear not to want to work as much as they did before.[27]

While in the city I had the pleasure of seeing some of my friends there whom I very much esteem. For the first two weeks the weather was unusually stormy which prevented my going out on any account. I made a visit to Bro. Rose's in company with Mrs. H. (Mr. H. being absent) and there met quite a company of interesting brethren and sisters—the Ive's family from Philadelphia and Sister Streper that I knew in St. Louis with others. I was much pleased with Sister Rose.

William Reed, James Nelson, and Thomas Clark left Manti on September 30, 1853, with a load of wheat. Isaac Morley and a horse company were to overtake the four men and go together through Salt Creek Canyon. Instead of camping near present-day Moroni, as agreed, the four men went on to Uintah Springs (Fountain Green). When Morley's party came upon the camp they found three dead men. Clark's body was found later under the wheat. Morley and the others "skirmished" with some Indians near Nephi, killing eight of them. A similar, less detailed account was published in the *Deseret News* of October 15, 1853. Martha implies that the Indians were shot in cold blood as revenge rather than as part of any "skirmish."

[26] The idea of having every settlement "fort up" became almost an obsession with Brigham Young during this unsettled period. All through the southern part of the territory, outlying ranchers and people in the smaller settlements were ordered to abandon their homes and move to larger centers. Settlements such as Nephi were built up. At the LDS church conference in October 1853, Heywood had been told to take fifty new families to Nephi to strengthen that town. In the *Deseret News* of December 1, 1853, George A. Smith could report that "Nephi musters about 100 men, and their fort is nearer completion than any other. They have a grist mill in operation, and a new school-house 20 by 40, nearly completed."

[27] The Walker War was over by May 1854.

I called over to Sister Vilate Kimball's and was much surprised to see the change in her. She is growing old fast.[28] Attended the Council house one day as visitor and heard a lecture from Bro. Kimball and was renewed in my mind in reference to the ordinances that I passed through three years ago. One thing pleased me, it was that all Bro. Kimball's wives were dressed in home made flannel and one other circumstance grieved me. Sister Vilate Kimball had received a letter from her Brother and his wife in Rochester denouncing the heads of this Church as wicked men, fearing lest my friends should feel the same.

April 16, 1854—Sunday—News from conference is of an interesting nature. Many of our brethren are nominated for various missions to the States, Canada and other countries. Erastus Snow to St. Louis to reside, Orson Pratt and Orson Spencer to Cincinnati, James Ferguson to Ireland, Brothers Sly and Gustin of this place to Canada and right to the town where my brother lives and also Bro. Sly expects to visit Rochester and I have given him letters accordingly.[29]

Brother Jeremiah Hatch has located with us to supervise the Indian Farm by appointment. He is a young man that I have much respected for his intellectuality and I have faith to believe he will be a blessing to this settlement.

April 23—Sunday—Mr. Heywood arrived here on Thursday afternoon—20th—on which day Bro. Rist commenced plastering our rooms which will add much to our comfort and at the same time commenced a steady rain such as we have not had since we settled in this place and to all appearance will save much labor in irrigating.

I did not attend the forenoon meeting at which time Mr. H. lectured the people pretty thoroughly on cleanliness, etc. etc.

April 24th—Monday—Rain continued very steady all day and night which prevented our men working in the field and instead thereof worked heartily in clearing away our chip piles and filth from out the Fort and will give the people a start to keep their door yards in better order. There is a disposition on the part of the peo-

---

[28] She would be forty-eight on June 1, 1854, not too many years older than Martha.

[29] James C. Sly, who had been cut off from the Mormon church for opposing Heywood so vigorously a year earlier, was back in the fold and presumably living in harmony with the Heywoods.

ple to have me teach school. Mr. H.'s health is not very good. I also begin to feel the influence of the weather and the damp of our rooms.

Bro. Siler [?] passed through and preached here on his way to the States where [he] is to fill his appointed mission. He is filled with a good spirit and his preaching was remarkably adapted to the wants of our people at this time.

Our gates were made and put up today which helps to prepare for Indian difficulties.

May 1st—Monday—Election of the city officers took place today and was a means to try the spirits of our people in regard to obeying council. Mr. Heywood as the president of this settlement filled the ticket but the people did not honor it. They took it upon themselves to make one to suit their notions and they carried the day. The most important change in the tickets was Bro. Foote for Mayor on the opposition ticket instead of Bro. Baxter and was what made the difficulty.

Our girls had their May walk and their picnic refreshment on their return to Sister Gifford's house as the Council House was used for election purposes.

Amelia Fellows has been working for me for a few days.

May 4th—Thursday—This being the first Thursday in the month was set apart for fasting and prayer. I attended the forenoon and afternoon meetings and felt much benefited thereby. There was quite a good attendance of females and Bro. Bigler presided, who with Bros. R. Carpenter and Nugent were the only brethren that attended.[30] We had a special prayer in behalf of Bro. Heywood's health and when he returned home I found him considerably better. Yesterday had Patriarchal blessings from Bro. Cazier to whom we made a visit and enjoyed ourselves very much.[31]

May 7th—Sunday—Yesterday Walker, the Indian Chief of the Utes made his appearance and put up to Brother Bradley's where Mr. Heywood met him with the brethren who are in authority in this place. Walker had six Indians with him. They partook of an entertainment got up for them and appeared to have a very good spirit indeed. Walker professed to be decidedly for peace. He had his patriarchal blessing from Father Cazier and a very good one it

[30] Jacob G. Bigler presided as bishop. The other two men, who have not been identified, may have been relative newcomers to the town.

[31] William and John Cazier were among the first Nephi settlers and were early town officials, councilor and treasurer respectively. See McCune, *History of Juab County,* pp. 56, 61.

was, provided he learned of the Mormons, to do as they do, to cultivate the earth, etc. etc.

A blessing was put upon the Indian Farm by Father Cazier on Wednesday, May 3rd.[32]

May 14th, 1854—Sunday—Wednesday afternoon Brother Brigham Young and his company arrived in our midst and in a little while entered our dwelling to refresh themselves.[33] Brother Young and wife Emeline; Kimball and wife, Lucy; Lorenzo Young and wife; Joseph and Phineas Young and others supped and breakfasted with us and seemed to enjoy themselves right well.[34] Had a meeting in the school house. Brother Brigham spoke and one of his remarks was that if the people did not obey counsel in building their Fort and wall and securing themselves they could get their throats cut. Parley Pratt and his company were in the crowd on their way to their mission ground.

After Bro. Brigham left here the spirit of the people was made manifest by their strenuously opposing Mr. Heywood in his counsel (if any) in reference to the building of the wall and insisted that Brigham's counsel (if any) was to build a fort. There was much hard feeling expressed on the subject towards Mr. H. and went so far as to say he was on the eve of apostacy.

Mr. Heywood's health was poor from the time he arrived here until this spirit manifested itself and then he felt somewhat better.

Commenced my school on Monday, May 15th with 27 scholars and in the afternoon of the same day Sisters Julia Leroy and Henricks [?] arrived which was a great advantage to me as I hardly knew what to do for help.

May 26th—Friday—Brother Brigham and his company arrived here on their way home from visiting the southern settlements.

---

[32] A list of names was entered in the diary at this point with no explanation. Perhaps they were the ones who opposed—or supported—Heywood. The names were: Bradley, Baxter, Bentley, Hart or Hayes, Hatch, Mangum, Spencer, Udall, T. Adair, E. Adair, Barber, Broadhead, Scofield, Carter, Finly, Henroid, Vickars and wife, John Wygle, Nutte, Sister LeRoy, Henroid, Scriggins, Micks, Harry Micks, Henry ————, David Cook, Rice, Bennett, William Cazier, Susanna Sly.

[33] Young and his party were on a four-week round trip from Salt Lake City to Harmony. At Chicken Creek (Levan) on May 11, Walker and other chiefs joined the tour. While Young was still urging caution and the building of forts and walls, the Walker War had come to a close; Indian missions and farms were planned, and "all the talks were favorable to a *good peace.* . . ." See *Deseret News,* May 25 and June 8, 1854.

[34] Members of the party included Emmeline Free Young, Lucy Walker Kimball, and the younger and two older brothers of Brigham Young: Lorenzo, Joseph, and Phineas.

They arrived in a storm of rain and continued to rain hard on the evening and night. They held a meeting. Brothers Hunter, Taylor and others spoke to the people. Brothers Brigham, Kimball and wives ate supper with us and remained all evening and night. They held a meeting.

Next morning the company started taking for their route, the other side of the western mountains. Mr. Heywood started with them for the city, leaving me to take care of quite a family. The enjoyment of the President and those of his company that accepted the hospitality that this humble roof afforded was truly gratifying to me.

Sabbath after the Presidency started, attended meeting in the afternoon, Bro. Kendall was the principal speaker.[35]

The brethren who accompanied the Presidency party to help to improve the road returned about noon, bringing the word that the wall was to be built and to be completed in three months, twelve feet high, 6 feet at the base to taper to two feet at the top.

June 15, 1854—Monday—On this day the brethren commenced the wall with vigor and unity and by their so doing my mind was exercised in reference to the similarity of our situation to that of the ancient Jews and I thought several times I would get the Bible and read the portion and see for myself the application to our circumstances and I was yet more interested on reading at its adaptness.

Walker on seeing the wall go up demanded what it was for and on being told it was to preserve ourselves from the Americans who were displeased with us for having more wives than one, he appeared satisfied with the explanation and Batiste desired that there would be a gate left for his special use on the southeast corner so that he might come in and out as he pleased.

On Saturday evening, June 10th. Walker [36] went to Bro. Bradley and told him the wall should not go up that it was not as he had told him to keep the Americans out, it was to keep him and his party out, that it was made known by a Mormon white boy to one of the Indian boys and that Brigham was coming here by and by to decoy him into our midst and cut off his head. He told him that if the wall went up our people would not gather their crops, that they would be destroyed. In consequence the wall had to be stopped and an express sent to Brigham.

---

[35] George Kendall, a seventy. See *Deseret News*, April 13, 1854.

[36] That the Mormons continued to "fort up" despite the recent peace settlement may have confused the wily Walker.

June 22nd—Thursday—We had a very good prayer meeting.

July 14th—Friday—Mr. Heywood accompanied by Sister Vary and Mary Bell arrived here, a few days previous Gustavus Henroid.

July 16th—Sabbath—We all attended meeting and Mr. H. was in good spirits and spoke as the spirit moved him and in the winding up of his remarks said he felt pretty well himself and asked the folks how they were—an expression that some took exception to. In the afternoon Father Miller[37] made a general confession which Mr. H. backed and this made matters worse.

During the week there was considerable excitement and Mr. H. was very much prostrated in strength of body. Also on Monday morning the school hour was missed which called out some remarks from Bro. Bryan as one of the trustees, that caused me to speak to him at noon time when I learned that there was considerably hard feelings against me as a school teacher. On my reporting to Mr. H. he desired me to ask them to liberate me which I did and closed the school, being about eight weeks of the quarter.

July 23rd—Sabbath—This Sabbath strength was given to Mr. H. to attend meeting and perform his duties as president of this place. It was not very well attended and on Tuesday morning following he left. When the excitement grew stronger and stronger and resulted in a petition been got up to remove Mr. H. from his office and while this was going on there was a remonstrance got up at the same time to the petition—the latter going a week ahead of the other and the answer being brought here by Bro. Bradley while the petition was on its way. The message was that Mr. H. was to rest and the people were to choose a president in whom they could be suited and when Father Miller and Bro. Foote returned they found the message was ahead of them.[38]

July 30th—Sabbath—I commenced to wean my girl without sufficient reflection. She took the weaning very well till about the fourth day when she was taken with diarrhea which I checked but she continued growing worse in a most astonishing manner. She was progressing in the cutting of a tooth which she brought through when I realized how hard it was going with her. I put her to the

---

[37] Probably Josiah Miller.

[38] How typical this is of a small settlement divided—bitter medicine for Martha.

breast again at which time she suffered herself so much that she would not touch it for two days.

On Tuesday, August 8th, the first return of her natal day I was very much concerned for her as she was very low indeed and when I wrote on Thursday, 10th, I had no encouragement for my self or her father. About two hours after the letter had gone I perceived a change for the better that grew brighter, slowly but steadily. Saturday the 5th, Sister Vickars buried her little girl that was born about the same time as mine.[39]

August 13th—Sabbath was appointed to elect a President and Bro. Kendall devised the plan which was to have all the candidates on paper and to get the marks of the people for 1st, 2nd and 3rd choice. Bishop Bigler received the majority of eight votes over Bro. Foote and was accordingly held up to the people to sustain which was done, but far from being unamimous. Mr. Heywood was presented previous and nearly a third voted for him. Bro. George Spencer demanded to know what Bro. H. had done, since Bro. Benson had settled the difficulty. Father Miller said he could tell and satisfy the people of the right of removing him which was hoped no dirty dog would unbury the hatchet. Bro. Carpenter was the first,[40] Bro. Bradley next and Bro. Heywood capped the climax by doing as he did the first Sabbath of his return. Bro. Spencer rose again and said Mr. Carpenter was opposed to Mr. H. when he did so and the last item called capping the climax was Bro. H. bearing testimony to Father Miller's confession. Bro. Bigler rose up and said that they had not come there to find fault with either party but the business of the day was to elect a President. So they accordingly attended to that business and when Bishop Bigler was duly pronounced President he rose up very smilingly and thanked the people for making him twice president in one day.

The subject of his required two counselors extra of the two he had in the Bishopric—and he gave it as his opinion that he needed them not, that the two offices were so intimately connected that except presiding at the meetings his duties would be as usual. He could not see that there was one hairs difference between the offices —he would even split the hair and say there was not that much difference. Bro. Bryan was voted in unanimously as first counselor

[39] John Vickers and his family had settled in Nephi during the summer of 1852. McCune, *History of Juab County,* p. 59.

[40] William H. Carpenter, a seventy. See *Deseret News,* April 13, 1854.

but Bro. Bently was questioned in regard to his office as clerk which called out some remarks from him. That he never sought the office but when it was given him he filled it to the best of his ability, not because he wanted it but because it was put upon him and he had always made it a principal to obey those who were set in authority over him and when he got ready to do otherwise than that he wanted to leave Mormonism.

October 1854—Sisters Julia and Henrietta started with Bro. Foote to attend conference. Sister H. returned [with] the wife of Bro. Love and Sister Julia took up her abode to Bro. Bryan's. And Bro. and Sister Broadhead, having previously left the house I found myself relieved of much company and the feeling of having much to do and my little girl quite poorly, I had to shoulder the burden with the assistance of Mary Anne Scriggens who added considerably to my cares.

About this time the Presidency passed through on their way to San Pete and to my surprise they were not long in the Fort till they honored me with a call. I was quite unprepared to entertain them but I went at it and soon provided a supper. Brother Brigham and his wife Emily Partridge ate supper to Bro. Bigler's but came over immediately after, remained for the evening and lodged over night and ate breakfast next morning. Bros. Kimball, Grant and others ate supper and breakfast and on their return from San Pete had the pleasure of entertaining the same company.[1]

[1] Brigham Young's party left Salt Lake City on October 10, 1854, to investigate the "unwise conduct of some foolish Indians in Utah, Juab, and San Pete counties" and to talk with those involved. "The notorious Washear, or Squash-head," promised to amend his behavior and was given a blanket by Young. See *Deseret News,* October 19 and 26, 1854. Young's skill as a diplomat is revealed in Martha's account of this visit. The president and his wife dined with Jacob G. Bigler, bishop and successor to Heywood in the office of president, and then returned to the Heywood household.

Immediately after, Mr. Heywood on his way to Iron Co. accompanied by Judge Stiles and others tarried one night as also on his return.[2]

The first night of the Presidency stay there was a meeting in which Brothers Kimball, Grant, Orson Hyde, preached to the people in reference to their recent movement of petitioning their president out and electing another in his place but the preaching was not understood by those who took part in the celebrated movement.

Commenced school second Monday in December with about twenty scholars which I found to be of much benefit to me as the activity of the operation and its responsibility prevented lonesomeness that otherwise would have been disagreeable.

Just at this time Mary Anne Scriggens left me which I realized to be a great blessing tho I endeavored to have her father leave her longer for the benefit of schooling but he would not and it seemed as if the Lord had said "I had borne enough."

A curious circumstance occured as touching a letter which was very lengthy relating to local matters of this place that I particularly wished to be private in our family, and given by me to Bro. Love, as I thought on his way to the city; but going no further than Dry Creek he passed it to Bro. Wright. It was found on the public road by Cottonwood by Bro. Stout who was journeying in company with Mr. Heywood on their trip South to Iron County and happened to leave the carriage for a walk and thereby found the letter.[3]

On the last day of November, and two following days, the people of Nephi celebrated the completion of this city, tho that completion was yet in an incipiant state and voted the same celebration to be held annually in room of the former annual feast instituted by their former President, J. L. Heywood, to celebrate the first starting of the surveying of Salt Creek, the first step in embryo of building up the city Nephi.[4]

[2] George P. Stiles succeeded Zerubbabel Snow as associate justice of the territory on August 1, 1854. The judicial party consisted of Stiles, Heywood, and Hosea Stout, U. S. attorney pro tem, and a posse of seventeen for protection through Indian country. There was little business for the U.S. Third District Court at Parowan to conduct, although twenty-five persons were sworn in as citizens. See Tullidge, *History of Salt Lake City*, p. 95, and *Deseret News*, January 4, 1855. The trip is also described in Brooks, *On the Mormon Frontier*, under November 9, 1854, and succeeding entries.

[3] A classic example of the hazards of sending mail by private hands.

[4] The immediate occasion of celebration was the completion of the disputed wall. The gates were hung and locked on the night of November 18, and November 30 and December 1 and 2 were appointed for feasting, music, speeches, toasts, and dancing. One account says that most of the citizens were rebaptized

Dancing, school, weekly calls, feasting and visiting continued all winter with an unsparing hand, as also an unusual liveliness in religious devotion in the public meetings, illustrating the joy and satisfaction taken by the people in the change wrought of the presidency of Nephi and a few isolated speeches descriptive that tyranny was at an end and the brethren rejoiced in their freedom.

Mr. Heywood started from his home in the city, May 16th, for Carson Valley and California[5] and previously made a trip to this place in his official character as U. S. Marshall of the Territory and disbursed some thousands of dollars in ready cash among the people relative to the U. S. Court held here by Judge Kinny and U. S. Attorney Holman, the most important case being the trial of the Indians for the murders of Gunnison and party—Coln. Steptoe, his officers and soldiers being also here to assist.[6]

Just previous to the breaking up of the court and while liquor was plenty, there was a debauch celebrated by some of the Gentile exquisites of both parties, to wit—military and judicial. The subjects were some squaws who were known by their lawful owner to have the power of transmitting disease to the said exquisites and the circumstance boasted of by the Indian (who was Ammon) all over the settlement.

During the time of court my little Nealy was very sick with fever. I had Doctor Hunt attend him who gave him some Calomel— that his fever, which had [been] on him for three weeks previous and could not [be] affect[ed] with anything I could give him.

May, the first part, of 1855—Had the pleasure of entertaining Bro. Brigham and such, on their way South. Brigham had his wife

for their sins prior to the celebration. See the letters of "Philomen" and Jacob G. Bigler in the *Deseret News* of November 30, 1854, and January 18, 1855.

[5] Heywood, Judge George P. Stiles, and Orson Hyde, on orders from the territorial assembly of 1854–55, were sent to Carson Valley to establish the boundary between Utah Territory and California. See Tullidge, *History of Salt Lake City*, p. 113.

[6] Capt. John W. Gunnison and seven of his party were killed by Indians on October 26, 1853, while camped on the Sevier River to survey a proposed route for the transcontinental railroad. The following spring Col. Edward Jenner Steptoe and a detachment of three hundred were sent to Utah to investigate the massacre. The trial of the three indicted Indians surrendered by Kanosh began in Nephi on March 21, 1855, under Chief Justice John F. Kinney. Joseph Hollman was prosecuting attorney and Almon W. Babbitt counsel for the defense. Jacob G. Bigler was jury foreman, and other settlers from Nephi and nearby towns served on the jury. Martha's description of the intemperate drinking and other questionable activities of soldiers and court officers is echoed by other eyewitnessnes. An excellent treatment of the subject is found in David Henry Miller, "The Impact of the Gunnison Massacre on Mormon-Federal Relations: Colonel Edward Jenner Steptoe's Command in Utah Territory, 1854–1855" (M. A. thesis, University of Utah, 1968).

Zina Huntington. Enjoyed the pleasure of her society very much. Bro. Kimball, his wives, Christiana and Anna.[7]

Brother Brigham again gave me the pleasure of waiting on their return from the south, eating supper with me and passing along to camp at the twelve mile springs and also giving me the invitation to follow them up and journey with them to the city as previously intimated,[8] which I did, starting from this place about four o'clock Saturday morning and joining in with the company to breakfast at Petit Neet, house of B. F. Johnson, and arriving Sunday morning in Salt Lake City between eight and nine o'clock to breakfast, a distance of 92 miles.[9] Found the Heywood family all well and glad to see me.

The rapid travelling, exposure to the night air and excitement previous to starting conspired to weaken my system so that I felt very poorly for a week or two after I arrived but my children were uncommonly well. Mrs. Heywood kind and affectionate and the whole family attending to my wants made me a very pleasant visit of about two months in Salt Lake City when I made a business of visiting and seeing my friends.

Before I left the city I imparted the rudimental ideas of hat trimming to Mrs. Heywood and Mary, also Sister Anna Ivans, to be improved upon at a future period. The hatting business is on a fair way to prosper as the person whom Mr. Heywood has given it to, Brother Merrill, seems to all appearances judicious and capable to carry it on. His sister (wife of Orson Pratt) has done the trimming heretofore but now it will be done by our folks.[10]

[7] Probably Christeen Golden and Ann Gheen.

[8] Brigham Young and party had left Salt Lake City on May 8 to visit the southern settlements and talk with Indians along the way. In the group were Garland Hurt, Indian agent, and interpreter D. B. Huntington. Dr. Samuel Sprague found the settlers in generally excellent health and was able to help the ailing Kanosh with some medicine. Another member of the party, Judge J. F. Kinney had come to "inspect the road made on contract with Col. Steptoe." According to Daniel Mackintosh, all was not business: Wilford Woodruff "has enjoyed himself along, angling; at which he exhibits much skill and patience. It is but fair to say he duly paid his tithing of two fish to Prests. Young and Kimball, to-day." A large seam of coal was inspected in Sanpete County, and Young learned enough of the problems of producing iron to reassure himself that the Iron Mission brethren were not lax in their work. Upon his return to Salt Lake City, the church president praised the value of families taking excursions together for their health and good cheer. He invited all who were able to go "without interfering with their business" to accompany him on his visits to the settlements. See *Deseret News,* May 9, 23, 30, 1855.

[9] How exciting to travel the ninety-two miles in less than thirty hours!

[10] During her time in Salt Lake City Martha laid the foundation for a good hat-manufacturing business by training some of the family in the basics of producing and trimming ladies' hats.

Returned to Nephi by stage. One in the company was G. A. Smith whose society I enjoyed much, staying to his house in Provo and continued our travel to Petit Neat and as usual stopped to Benjamin Johnson's.

July 20th—Friday—On my returning I found my house and its contents all safe but very full of dust. Spent next day cleaning and putting to rights and in so doing I realized a remarkable improvement in my physical strength. And as I had predetermined to keep a select school I gave it out accordingly. I found that several of the scholars I had depended on were signed to Bro. Love, he having gone round the settlement the day previous to my getting here.[11] There were a few who urged me to commence my school and I did so the following Monday morning with 17 scholars but could easily sense the general opposition to my doing so.

Soon after my return I was made acquainted with the determined opposition to Bro. Meeks by his brethren of the Seventies to his being their President.[12] They seemed to loathe the man with perfect disgust and in consequence got up a petition against him charging him with many things that I felt he was innocent of. Brethren Bigler, Kendall and Wm. Holden took the petition to the city with a view of presenting it to President Brigham Young. But according to the report given by Bro. Bigler to [a] public congregation in this place he felt as if he could not present it to him at least without first seeing Brother Joseph Young.[13] So they went to Joseph and accordingly to their united testimony Bro. Joseph gave them to understand that the reason he ordained Bro. Meeks was because Bro. Heywood had dogged them to it—that Bro. Wolf or Bro. Hatch would have been his choice.[14] I attended the meeting and was taken somewhat by surprise in hearing the remarks of the brethren not only condemning Mr. Heywood but slurring his character in any spirit but that of righteousness, proving him to be a liar by the remarks of Joseph Young and Bro. Foote added his testimony by saying that Mr. Heywood was in a Gentile office and acted in the spirit of a Gentile officer.

[11] Andrew Love and the other Clover Creek (Mona) residents had moved to Nephi during the Walker War. See McCune, *History of Juab County*, p. 138.

[12] William Meeks.

[13] Joseph Young, an elder brother of Brigham, was one of the first seven presidents of seventies, serving from 1835 to 1881. He traveled and preached extensively throughout the territory. See Jenson, *LDS Biographical Encyclopedia*, 1:187–88.

[14] John A. Woolf had been acting president of the seventies at Nephi the previous year. See *Deseret News*, April 13, 1854.

Brother Meeks was up before the people to be tried for his conduct and after the whole day was consumed in the investigation he was cut off from this branch, the leading charge was for keeping company with the disaffected—not bringing up his children properly, being idle, etc. etc. Bro. Jermiah Hatch was likewise before the ———— but confessed to anything they brought up that thereby he might not be cut off.[15]

Brethren Joseph Young, Horace Eldrich, Rockwood, came here to visit the seventies and to preach the gospel, not only to them but to the people and in addition to right up some things that were crooked.[16] To my inexpressible satisfaction they—[a pencil line has been run through this]—they called on me and on my inviting them consented to make it their home while they stayed with the exception of Bro. Rockwood who put up with the Bishop.

An interesting circumstance occured while I was simply conversing with Bros. Young and Eldridge, referring to the trial I passed through while hearing my husband proved a liar in the public congregation and that said to be on the testimony of what he, Bro. Young, said to the Bishop and George Kendall. Bro. Young at once denied saying that Bro. Heywood never influenced him in the matter of appointing Bro. Meeks and as he was talking on the subject he————.

On Friday, he, Mr. Heywood arrived here, November 6th, by horseback, being the first time I had seen him since his trip down here in March, being an absence of eight months.[17]

On Sunday he preached in the school house in the spirit of his office as Missionary and this being the first time he presented himself before the people since previous to his rejection by them as their President. I noticed the moral atmosphere and my observations convinced me that the feelings were below par towards him.[18]

Brother T. D. Brown,[19] being likewise one of the appointed missionaries, was of much assistance to Mr. Heywood in attempting

[15] Martha seemed skeptical of Hatch's "confession."

[16] Horace S. Eldredge and Albert P. Rockwood were both presidents of seventies, Eldredge serving in that capacity from 1854 to 1888 and Rockwood from 1845 to 1879. See Jenson, *LDS Biographical Encyclopedia*, 1:194–97. The crisis at Nephi must have been acute for three of the seven presidents of seventies to converge on the town.

[17] Heywood's "Gentile" duties as U. S. marshal kept him from Nephi for long periods, a fact that may have helped to undercut his position there.

[18] Heywood needed some courage to face the congregation that had rejected him, and Martha recognized that he was still not completely accepted.

[19] Brown was one of a large company of missionaries to the Indians in the southern part of the territory. Their headquarters was in the vicinity of Harmony

the task and but for him [he] would not have braved it as I had reason to think he took some cold on his journey here and a little more the night previous in bathing. My own health was poorly as also Sarepta was, suffering from a severe cold which quite prostrated her and made her feel rather peevish which caused her father to speak unkindly to her which was hurtful to my feeling, so that the three days he spent here were not quite as agreeable as I could wish and that after so long an absence.

December 24th—Received by George Spencer a letter from Mrs. Heywood informing me of Mr. H.'s poor health and also of his displeasure towards me in reference to my going ahead with work contrary to his instructions and also the spirit of writing, which has troubled me so seriously that all other trials and troubles seems but trifling.[20]

I have set my heart on attending more strictly to family directions. A desire to effect my children while young has sharpened my apprehension of this duty but I cannot but realize how much I have suffered perplexity and petty trials for weeks past and often try to account for the reason.

I rejoiced in the thought of Mr. H.'s getting Susan Sherman to come down to spend the winter with me and loved the girl and do love her yet, but my trial with her commenced before she was with me a week and I have faithfully tried to curb my temper and avoid scolding. And the making an extra effort to accomplish some work this winter has put me about considerable with my poor health. But I realize it is but another link of the chain and the result of my oft meditation is that it is one of the many means necessary for my future exaltation and provided by a kind providence. My little daughter has quite recovered and both children are in apparent good health and very interesting and to me they are truly the bright spot of many a clouded season.

January 1st, 1856—Washed all day to commence the New Year. Susan Sherman who has been on a visit with me for the last two or three weeks has been quite a trial to me, so determined to follow her disposition to run all the time. Lizzy Meeks left me last Friday and I have concluded not to have her any more as her mother

and took in the area south to the Santa Clara. Brown's journal is most eloquent of the life and culture of these Indians. See Juanita Brooks, ed., *Journal of the Southern Indian Mission: Diary of Thomas D. Brown* (Logan: Utah State University Press, 1972).

[20] Martha was very sensitive to criticism from her husband.

is determined to frustrate all the good I try to do her. During the last few weeks I have suffered in my mind exceedingly and believe it to be one of those trials "That must and will arise to every human breast." And if I have but grace not to sin the unpardonable sin I can lay hold of the anchor of hope and hold on till the storm is over. May God of his infinite love have mercy on my weakness and give me strength according to my day.

January 3rd—Thursday—This morning Sister Wright came to borrow the lounge for the convenience of Bro. Wright who cut his foot on the morning of the first of New Year's day while chopping wood. As Susan had slept on it I felt much hesitancy in loaning it but Sister Wright so overrulled this objection by arranging with Susan to sleep with her that I was obliged to refer the matter to Susan and of course the lounge was taken for Bro. Wright's accommodation and I could not regret it as he suffered keenly though I was afterwards censored by Mr. Heywood for letting it go; he considering that Susan might take advantage of my doing so for leaving the house, which she did that day.

Mr. and Mrs. Heywood arrived on their way to Fillmore with a large amount of judicial officers, attendants, etc., as also Bro. Babbitt.[21] I was glad he came just at this time on Susan's account. He preached in the school house in the evening and also some of the home missionary brethren.

Mr. and Mrs. Heywood tarried next day as also the whole company who were quartered round to different places. They all started next morning on route to Fillmore after preparing abundantly for their camping arrangements.

This flying call of Mr. H.'s was of considerable comfort to me, and I at once (when he arrived, which was unexpected) made up my mind to make the most of the interview to make right little things that had the appearance of being wrong which I believed was in a measure explained away.[22]

January 19, 1856—Brother Brigham and Legislative Company passed through on their way home to the city. Arrived here about

---

[21] The supreme court was scheduled to begin its session in Fillmore on Monday, January 7, 1856. Since the court officers arrived in Nephi on a Thursday, a day of fasting for the town, they were served "a nice dish of sucketash in the evening. . . ." See Erastus Snow's letter in the *Deseret News* of January 23, 1856.

[22] Keenly conscious of her husband's coolness and criticisms, Martha was always on the defensive.

ten and tarried about three hours. Bros. Brigham, Kimball, their wives and others connected with them ate breakfast to my preparing. Just as they drove off Mr. and Mrs. Heywood and company arrived. They stayed over night.[23] I had a pleasant interview with them. Mr. H. left sundry directions with me, refering to my leaving here to reside in the city for a season. His health seemed much improved since he left here two weeks previous.

After my husband and his wife Sarepta left me, I felt a spirit of peace that I enjoyed to my hearts content and a desire and determination to rise above the petty circumstances that were continually bearing upon my mind. I also felt, at times, agreeable at the thought of removing to the city for a season. I set myself to get some sewing done and felt a pleasure in it. I even fancied or felt a pleasure, or a spirit that many of the people who appeared so unfriendly to me were repenting of it. Bro. Bigler's wife Amy, has been very sick indeed but after taking an Emmetic she recovered very fast and during her state of convalescence I had an opportunity of showing my good feelings towards her. Bro. Wolf's little boy William was taken sick with what appeared to me to be the measles but Bro. Bryan called it Scarlet Fever.

About this time I was much tried on the subject of breaking up housekeeping in Nephi and taking my furniture to the City to keep house there. I made some faint endeavors to overcome my reluctance and in a measure became reconciled but not perfectly. Mary Gustin called in on her return from the city giving me a verbal message from Mrs. H. that if my children were taken with the measles to give them Saffron tea or bran water. Learned from her Joseph came as far as Provo and did not send me one single word which hurt my feelings and taught me to think that I was not much cared for; Mary having stayed three days in the house and journeyed with him to Provo. I felt there was no possible reason but he might have sent me a few lines, not having but one letter from him during the whole winter and that one when he was in Filmore. I try to recognize the hand of the Lord in all of this for the perfecting of my character but as Paul says, "Afflictions for the present are grievous but afterwards they yield the peaceable fruits of righteousness to them who are excerted thereby." And to know how lavish he has been all this winter, and so stringent towards me and my health so poorly

---

[23] Brigham Young's party arrived back in Salt Lake City on January 21 and the court party on the following day. See *Deseret News*, January 23, 1856.

all winter is a trial for a woman that has so little stamina as I have got.[24] I would I could overcome my own weakness and enjoy the blessings I do possess and let the rest go for naught.

---

[24] Martha had been on her own most of the time in Nephi, making hats and teaching for a living in a community that was sharply divided in its feelings toward her husband. Her bitterness at Joseph's apparent neglect is understandable.

February 22, 1856—Nealy was taken sick in the morning, complained of sore mouth, headache, had several diarrhea passages during the day and threw up phlegm twice or thrice, breath smelt very bad of canker. Doctored at once for the canker and also gave him some Saffron and sage tea. Next day continued very sick and showed some rash, fever very high. Towards night I bathed him all over with Salerates water and the rash or measles came out very full, so I continued to give him Saffron tea and sage. He was very sick and took a turn on Tuesday (26th) for the better and that evening my dear little Sarepta came down with the same rash but appeared to have no canker. Having four nights watching with Nealy and he on the gain I relaxed my efforts in sitting up at night, not thinking that there was any particular danger in my dear little girl's case until she was sick one week—March 4th. Then I began to realize her real state which was dangerous to say the least. I called on Bro. Bryan to see her and he gave his opinion that canker was in her stomach and the rash had turned in and desired me to give her the canker medicine and to try to get the rash out. He would not allow that it was measles. I did my best by bathing her in Salerates water, gave her Saffron tea to drink but it seemed to strike it in the more. She seemed to be some better which made my heart glad but in about two days she relapsed again and with the change sorrow again filled my heart. I went to Sister Bently's for lobelia as I realized the chief difficulty lay in her breathing and not in canker but having given her canker medicine that had blue Vitriol in it it was not wise to give her the Lobelia. I gave her Caster Oil and annointed her plentifully with consecrated oil and gave her some inwardly.

On Wednesday the 12th of March I first gave her the Lobelia in doses of tincture. It was several hours in her system without operating. I gave her rhubarb to work it off which she did and passed some phlegm and at this time I had discovered the hard phlegm stuck to her mouth and was more convinced that the difficulty lay in her chest. She again took a turn for the better after this first administered Lobelia and my spirits again revived. She seemed easier Thursday night when I went to bed and being very much exhausted I fell into a heavy slumber and woke up by her calling to me and when I had come to myself I found her in very great distress with her breathing. I had some onions and I put them under her arms and oiled her well. Went after Sister Bigler that she might assist me in putting her feet in water. It was two o'clock when she came in and we bathed her feet which seemed to ease her breathing a little but until daylight she appeared to be dying but between six and seven she revived again which comforted me much. As I had had a night of keen anguish my hopes revived much during the day, although she was quite feeble and low. Louisa Barber watched that night and encouraged to hope which continued till next night when I had again to weep over her as dying. Adeline was with me who had a hard time of it. She was so restless and suffering I determined that if she lived till I could give her a regular lobelia emmetic I would try it (knowing that she could not live without having the phlegm removed). About twelve o'clock I gave her the emmetic which opperated well in her system but about four o'clock she had the appearance of dying and I again gave her up. Oh, my poor heart, how it was wrung with anguish but again she revived and called "Mamma" which word once more heard made me crazy with joy which continued till she was really death struck and the only thing to desire or hope for was to have her Father come in time to see her once again and he did arrive on Tuesday, 18th, about six o'clock in the evening. She had been dying all day and the night before and when he came she stretched her little arms to him and called Papa and all that night would call to sit on Papa's lap. She died next morning about eight o'clock, being sensible to the last breath she could draw and [when she] ceased to breath the bad smell ceased. I washed her little body myself on my lap and dressed her in her own clothes and the last sewing I did for her was to make her a pair of shoes of white cloth.

Oh, my dear little Sarepta Marie my joy and my comfort by day and by night. Your precious voice that so often cheered my heart to its inmost recesses by its singing and interesting prattle, had gone from my sight. And I fully realized the goodness of the Lord by his providence to permit her Father to see her before she ceased to live in this present state of existence and that I was permitted to have his company during the funeral rites.

After retiring that night with my husband and my little boy I felt dreadful lonesome and anticipating how much worse it would be after [I] would lose sight of the little that remained of her. I asked my husband if it were possible if I could accompany him on his journey to the city as he was obliged to start after the burial. He thought he could work it so that I could, so I put a few things together in a hurry in the morning and started leaving the house and all belonging to it in the care of Sister Vickers and then started with our dear little girl's remains, to bury her out of our sight. It was the first time I had ever been to the burial ground of Nephi.[1]

We had the gratification of the presence of Brother Erastus Snow whose remarks of the subject of death seemed more lucid than I had ever heard at a previous funeral occasion. He drew such a plain comparison between the child being born into this world giving joy and satisfaction to its parents and friends, so in the spirit leaving its former abode and companions there was regret in departure. So in like manner when a spirit leaves us we sorrow at its departure but they rejoice. His remarks were very comforting and in his prayer there was a power of intelligence that interested me much.

We forenooned at the 12 miles Springs. There was in the company Erastus Snow, Levi Hancock and Bishop Charles Hancock, Jackson Stewart,[2] my husband, self and little boy. We ate our biscuit and butter with thankfulness and proceeded on our journey and arrived in Petit Neat at sundown. The conversation was instructing and interesting. Levi Hancock[3] told his dream which he had the night before and it was this wise: He was in company with

---

[1] No comment can enhance the plain, heartfelt eloquence of Martha's own writing.

[2] Andrew Jackson Stewart had been with William Huntington in 1854 on the Elk Mountain Mission (near Moab) when they had to take their wagons apart and lower them over the cliff piece by piece. See [Dale L. Morgan], *Utah: A Guide to the State* (New York: Hastings House, 1954), p. 424.

[3] Levi W. Hancock was one of the first seventies ordained by Joseph Smith in 1835 and soon became one of the first seven presidents of seventies, a position he held until his death in 1882. He was chaplain with the Mormon Battalion, an early settler at Manti, and a delegate to the legislative assembly. See Jenson, *LDS Biographical Encyclopedia*, 1:188–89.

Joseph Smith where there was a large assemblage of persons and Joseph Smith handed around to the company some liquor that looked like wine and some refused but when offered to him he at once took it and it was the most delicious exhilerating beverage, running through his system with avidity causing the most pleasurable feelings that could be imagined and [he] saw Joseph turn round and reprove those who refused and say, "It was always so with them, they would always refuse what he would give them and they were all rottenness and there was nothing in them."

The agreeable company and good conversation was calculated to draw me off my sorrowful feelings. We put up to David Lebanon and next morning ate breakfast to Bishop Hancock's[4] and resumed our journey and got into Provo in good season and put up to Bro. Redfield's.[5] I felt very poorly and had to lay down at once. Next morning we started with Brother Bullock and two sisters Bullock and arrived at Cottonwood between eight and nine o'clock at night and had some difficulty in finding a stopping place. We had a rest to Bro. Harrington's where we took up Bro. Snow and had a most desirable time in conversation.[6] We finally made out to stay to a Bro. Cox's humble roof—there were six of us.[7]

Next day, being Sabbath, there was notice (tho very short) to have preaching by the missionaries. I attended meeting and tho very poorly I enjoyed the spirit of the preaching and was stuck by the similar style of ideas and language in Erastus Snow and Brigham. After meeting by invitation we refreshed ourselves to Silas Richards' house and started immediately after to continue our journey.[8] Cottonwood settlement appeared to be in a flourishing condition and for size seemed the best started settlement as to compactness and good buildings that I have seen as yet.

Arrived about six o'clock in the evening to my husband's house in the city with my heart and in the reflections of my recent loss and my health so poorly. The family appeared to be all enjoying good

[4] Charles B. Hancock, an early settler on Peteetneet Creek (Payson), was bishop of the settlement. See Huff, *Memories that Live,* p. 434.

[5] Harlow Redfield was one of Provo's first aldermen. Ibid., p. 62.

[6] Leonard E. Harrington was the first bishop and postmaster of American Fork. He also served in the territorial legislature and the Nauvoo Legion. See Jenson, *LDS Biographical Encyclopedia,* 3:799–800.

[7] This could have been either John Cox, a counselor in the Little Cottonwood (Union) bishopric, or Jehu Cox, a settler who gave ten acres of his farmland for the fort site. See Kirkham and Lundstrom, *Tales of a Triumphant People,* pp. 263–67.

[8] Silas Richards, first bishop of the Little Cottonwood settlement, was also its first teacher and postmaster. He introduced peaches and grapes to the area from Dixie. Ibid.

health and the meeting was rather a sad one. I felt a chord of sympathy vibrate in the bosom of Sister Vary that was a testimony of better feelings towards me.

March 30, 1856—Sunday—Mr. H. started this morning on a preaching excursion as also to try to get some bread stuff as far north as Ogden taking his wife Mary and Archy her brother.[9] I attended meeting in the forenoon and heard preaching from a young son of Erin's Isle of the name of Patrick Lynch, giving a sketch of his bringing up which was in the bosom of the church of Rome. I enjoyed his remarks with a zest that was truly agreeable and all seemed to enjoy them very much. His bursts of witticisms caused much laughter.

In the afternoon I again attended the meeting tho very feeble. I was impressed that Bro. Brigham would preach and I was not disappointed and subjects of his remarks were of thrilling interest to me and I remarked to Sarepta as we left the house that my feelings were that I could not have missed hearing that sermon for all I had ever heard before. The subject of equality was splendidly handled by him as also that of love or the social affections. I was fairly drunk with enjoyment and the consciousness that I would have the pleasure of perusing it after publication is truly gratifying.

April 6th, 1856—Sunday—Conference commenced this morning in the Bowery which was comfortably fixed up for the accommodation [of a] very large concourse of people. The crowd was so dense and crowding so great that I was obliged to give up and return home and was not able to attend any more of the meetings during Conference.

April 13th—Sunday—Spent an afternoon to Sister Hiram Kimball's[10] in company with my Lord and his wife Sarepta; also Sisters Eliza Snow and Whitney. Joseph enjoyed himself well but is very slim. Next day visited to Bro. Merrill's all the family, not excepting the children.[11] Next day visited to Bro. Stout's with Joseph and Sarepta.[12]

[9] According to family genealogical records, Mary Bell received her endowments on March 31, 1854, and was sealed to Joseph on October 31, 1855. Their first child was not born until January 1858. In the meantime, they had adopted an Indian boy named Omer Badigee, born 1847.

[10] Hiram S. Kimball, a pioneer of 1850, was one of two missionaries to the Sandwich (Hawaiian) Islands in 1863 who were killed when the boiler of their steamer exploded. See Jenson, *LDS Biographical Encyclopedia*, 2:372.

[11] Which of several Merrills this might have been is not apparent from the text.

[12] The visit to Hosea Stout may have been as much business as pleasure. Heywood was preparing to leave for Washington, and on April 17, 1856, he gave Stout a certificate of appointment as U.S. deputy marshal. Stout said he

April 20th—Sunday—I realize that my health is improving some but did not attempt to go out of the house to meeting on account of the stormy weather. The rain that we are having seems to be present comfort if not salvation. Spent the day in assisting to make ready things for my husband's journey. As my health improves so does my mind gather strength. On Friday we three wives went through the ordinance of being sealed to our head or husband in the house of the Lord.[13] In the morning previous I had an errand to Sister Presinda Kimball and being very weak in body I asked if she felt like giving me a blessing which she did with alacrity, the substance of which was very comforting to me.[14] The run of it was that the Lord knew the integrity of my heart and that I would not do anything contrary to His will if I knew it; that he had his eye upon me for good and that the trials that I was passing through were for my good; that my boy would live to be a comfort and staff to old age and that the Lord would make all right with me in due season and I should have my true mate who would sympathize with my afflictions, etc. etc.

During the ceremony of the sealing I was struck with the fact that the first wife was not called upon to give away the other wives to her husband, but was asked if she was willing that he should take so and so to be his wife.

April 22nd.—Tuesday—Joseph seemed decidedly better yesterday and this morning than since we returned from Nephi. He started about nine o'clock in good spirits for the states in company with many of the twelve and other Elders on their various missions.[15]

did not intend to act in that office but would have charge of it during Heywood's absence "more to prevent abuse and extravagance than any thing else." See Brooks, *On the Mormon Frontier,* 2:595–96.

[13] This was the third ceremony Martha had been through. She was married in January 1851 and received her endowments three months later.

[14] Prescindia Huntington Kimball was a sister of Indian interpreter Dimick B. Huntington. A midwife, she was described as being "stately, gracious, and proportioned on heroic lines. She was a tower of strength in a sick room, and her very presence inspired courage and faith." See Carter, *Our Pioneer Heritage,* 10:391–92.

[15] Heywood would be gone for eleven months. The travelers were met by cold, wet weather, including severe blizzards in Wyoming. Heywood reached Washington on June 23. Little is known of his business there except that he probably had some official matters to discuss in his capacity as a U. S. marshal, and he planned to promote statehood. He was removed from office in August 1856, "seemingly because of a discrepancy in his financial accounts." The marshal's office was in debt $116,845.59 for expenses the government had refused to pay. Congress eventually authorized payment of Heywood's accounts in 1873. For a brief sketch of Heywood's activities as marshal see Vernal A. Brown, "The United States Marshals in Utah Territory to 1896" (M.S. thesis, Utah State University, 1970), pp. 11–25. Heywood's trip to Washington was also noted by Hosea Stout. See Brooks, *On the Mormon Frontier,* 2:596, 624.

April 27, 1856—Sunday—During the last week my health has been decidedly better and with this fact I realize an improvement in my mind and I have gained some towards a peaceful state of mind and hope to increase.

This forenoon attended meeting and heard Bro. Barnard Snow whom Brother Brigham called to the ———— preached his first sermon to the congregation and was very interesting and profitable. Obedience was the subject. And after his remarks Brigham followed him in the same channel but on an enlarged scale.

Before he spoke, supposing that he would, I prayed my Heavenly Father that I might get instruction that would suit my particular circumstances and I did feel that I did and had the very thing pointed out that I needed. And I prayed my Heavenly Father that I may receive it in honesty and that it may [make] an impression on my mind and more especially the principle that a woman be she ever so smart, she cannot know more than her husband if he magnifies his Priesthood. That God never in any age of the world endowed woman with knowledge above the man and when a woman has in any instance a message from God to man 'tis because of the Priesthood.[16]

This afternoon heard Bro. Lewis give a description of his mission to the islands of the sea which to me was very interesting.

———————

This morning I awoke remembering this much of a dream. I was somewhere where I had lived and was as it were remodeling the house and premises. There was a back house the woodwork of which seemed to be removed and I was mixing up the manure and dirt together, having it in my mind that it was to mix through the soil for the benefit of vegetation. I saw a neighbor's soil on his lot that looked most thrifty and I thought within myself how thrifty it was—there was grass growing on it and broken off at the edge of the lot which enabled me to see the soil. My brother Robert stood on the opposite side of the lot. Then I saw a part of a vine that looked some like a hop vine and it appeared as if it had made its way to my premises from that of another person's premises and I took hold of it and found two tendrils and had twined together and when I examined towards the root or where it started from, found that the stalk of the tendrils had formerly been injured and had the appearance of old rope and this appearance was about an inch in length

———

[16] This doctrine was hard for Martha to remember, since in many things she did know more than her husband.

and I noticed how the tendrils had grown so thrifty, the sap or life passing through the seemingly diseased part. In drawing the tendril along they had to pass, as it were, over two walls before they came to the window of my house and these two formed a little enclosure which appeared like a waste place and where the vine was growing appeared to be premises belonging to Sister Davis. I also thought that the vines when nailed on the house would make a handsome shade to my window.

A few nights ago I dreamed that I was in a road or place very familiar to me in my childhood days and I wished to go to a place a little further on named Ball's bridge but could not go.

ONCE MORE IN THE BOSOM OF
MY HUSBAND'S FAMILY

12

April 28th—Monday—Left the city with Bro. Merrill on an excursion as far south as Nephi to hunt up bread stuff and what other provisions we could get hold [of] for trade.[1] Arrived in Draperville at two o'clock and found Bro. Brown and his family packing up for Carson. Maryanne, formerly Bro. Kimball's wife, started with us for her home in Provo, having married a good man of the name of Walton.[2] I proposed to myself to be very taciturn so that I might not enlist my sympathies in her behalf which I carried out till after we left Draperville and by the time we arrived to Bishop Harrington's I found myself deeply interested in her recital of all the circumstances that caused her to leave Bro. Kimball.

Next morning before leaving we were blessed with a smart snow storm and were delayed till about ten o'clock in consequence. The weather was very inclement. Arrived in Provo about three o'clock and put up to Bro. Stewart's for the night. Remained in

---

[1] Zion was in the grip of a famine. Crops had failed, and winters had been severe. Many cattle had died. Even well-to-do families had to ration their grain through the winter of 1855–56. The poor suffered the most, of course, and only the "semi-patriarchal character of the community preserved thousands from perishing." See Tullidge, *History of Salt Lake City,* p. 113. A graphic description of the famine is given in the letter of Heber C. Kimball to his son William that Tullidge published on pp. 113–15.

[2] The only Mary Ann listed among Kimball's wives by Orson F. Whitney is Mary Ann Shefflin, but this is not she.

Provo next day which passed very lonesome as my thoughts were busy on my circumstances, more especially in the loss of the sweet society of my little girl. Spent the most of the day with Beans who were very kind to me. We learned that bread stuff was in Provo but hard to be got.

Arrived in Nephi the second of May in the afternoon and noticed some improvements, especially Cottonwood trees. The people seemed [happy] to see me and my grief for my little girl was taken from me and perhaps it was owing to my realizing how much sympathy was due to others and their sufferings in a measure greater than my own. When sitting with Sister Lucy Smith she opened the subject of the spirits being required in the world of spirits and related the circumstances of Sarah Smith who died about five years ago and left her boy whom Lucy took care of and one night when having her feelings drawn out considerable towards the child who was suffering from a cold, the mother came to her and Lucy asked her if she was happy and she said she was and that she was very busy, that she was all the time making temple clothes. She also told me how Brigham told father John Smith when on his death bed to tell Joseph that he was doing the best he could for this people and if he was not to let him know what he should do. The simplicity of the message pleased me. I enjoyed the company of Bro. Merrill during my ride very much. And now I am once more in the bosom of my husband's family and I am determined to do all I can for our mutual comfort and advantage.

May 11th, 1856—Sunday—Yesterday the eastern mail arrived in this place and we had by it the third letter from Joseph who is rapidly improving in his health and in good spirits.

Sister Vary very much prostrated by chills and fever.

May 17, 1856—Sunday—Sister Vary continues very feeble. Sat in the room during morning prayers. She is much prostrated. During the past week my health has been quite good and my mind enjoying that peace and happiness that is so desirable. My boy (who is now my only comfort) is gaining in health for which I feel grateful. On Monday we heard of the death of R. W. Woolcott, a missionary to England. He died there of the small pox. Our intimate acquaintance with his wife and himself caused us to feel as if he were one of our own family.

The Lord continues to bless us in not only the necessities of life but also the comforts. I got in my possession this week a daguerreotype taken two years and three months ago by Bro. Cannon—myself and two children which is now very precious to me and as a special providence.[3]

May 25th—Sunday—Nothing very special occured during the past week to us as a family. Sister Vary continues very low. Attended the "pollysophical" on Friday evening and heard my name called for a piece for the next week.

June 1st—Sunday—Last night I dreamed that I was travelling some road and saw two men and their horses as if they came a distance having that rough look that indicated the same and as I kept looking at them I realized the elder one was Brother Foote and the younger his son Guy. He came right up to me and appeared glad to see me and told me his [wagon] was right by, all loaded. I went along with him to where the wagon was and he assisted me in and I sat as it were on the edge of the front board conversing with him as to where he was going and if it were true that he had left Nephi and he assured me of the fact. Sister Foote was in the back part of the wagon and I spoke to her and asked if she was not very glad to go north to be near her sister (having heard from Bro. Foote that he was going north). She said she was and asked me if I would not go see her. I answered that I surely would. I asked Mr. Foote if Sarah had not died. He said she had not, she was alive. I told him I considered it then a miracle. They kept travelling along and I realized they were not going my road. I noticed that Sister Foote's hand was bound up in a cloth which reminded me of its being burned. I did not see Sarah. I then went where I was going which was like going into a basement and met the one I expected but whether it was Mrs. Hayes or Sarepta Heywood I did not distinctly understand. She had a calico print that I much admired as also the make of it and remarked that I wished I could get as good and pretty one. I told about Brother Foote and while telling it I remarked—I know you are not so much interested in it as I am but for my part I am greatly delighted in Brother Foote's leaving Nephi.

A few nights previous I dreamed of the Botty [?] horse getting in the house and my trying to get him out and others engaged in the same things. She was docile. The other mares seemed the first in the dream.

---

[3] Marsena Cannon was the first known resident photographer in Utah and the first to take daguerreotype portraits. He came to Utah in 1850 and for a decade was the most important photographer in the territory. His are the earliest photographs of Salt Lake City. See Nelson Wadsworth, "Zion's Cameramen: Early Photographers of Utah and the Mormons," *Utah Historical Quarterly* 40 (1972): 33–39.

This is the second dream I have had about horses. The former one was when the horses were running and I admiring their swiftness, etc. etc.

This morning attended meeting and heard a Bro. Smith just come from his mission in Africa. He spoke right well, seemed to possess a very good spirit. Brother Kimball spoke after.

Friday evening attended the Pollysophical and made my debut as a contributer.[4] The piece I read was that on my mother written some years ago.

My health is running down of late.

I have come to a decision this day—to quit drinking TEA. June 1st.

June 8th—Sunday—1856—I have to record that my resolution of not drinking tea has failed. My health was so miserable during ———— that I was tempted to take a cup Friday evening to enable me to attend the Pollysophical Society and since then have used tea fully and feel suprisingly better.

This forenoon attended the Bowery and was truly comforted and instructed by the preaching of Bros. Joseph Young, Kimball and Brigham. There were such a variety of good instruction that I feel unable to scan it.

Attended Ward meeting which consisted of business matters pertaining to the canal which is to fetch the waters of Big Cottonwood into the city.[5] The meeting was well attended and a good spirit and interest manifested.

Friday evening attended the Pollysophical which was well attended and Bro. Brigham, which is two evenings running on. On account of the lateness of the hour there was not many essays delivered but there was much music and singing.

June 15th—Sunday—Attended meeting this forenoon and heard Bro. Brigham who read a revelation given to the Church, Sec.

---

[4] The Polysophical Society was organized in 1854 at Lorenzo Snow's hall. The society's activities and its forced demise in October 1856 when reformation swept the church are discussed briefly in Maureen Ursenbach, "Three Women and the Life of the Mind," *Utah Historical Quarterly* 43 (1975): 28–29, 31–32.

[5] Ward members were probably discussing their contributions to this public works project. The proposed canal was to be used to freight granite for the temple into the city. This impractical scheme was abandoned with the coming of Johnston's army. See Wallace Alan Raynor, "History of the Construction of the Salt Lake Temple" (M.S. thesis, Brigham Young University, 1961), pp. 96–110.

18, concerning the appointing of Edward Partridge to the Land of
Zion, etc.[6] Bro. Brigham dwelt some on those who are commanded
and obey such commandments because they are commandments and
do not those things willingly in and of themselves are unprofitable
servants.

He also spoke of those who want revelations. Many may have
some given them before long but the revelation will be to cut them
off from the Church. He also spoke to the bishops about getting
acquainted with the families of their wards, seeing into their circumstances, etc. He related a circumstance about a child going round
begging under false circumstances, also of some woman being over-
heard telling of keeping their money and going to Brigham and
obtaining flour from him by making a good story.

June 19, 1856—Thursday—Three months today my dear little
Sarepta left this world of care and the love and embraces of a
mother who loved her with a fondness that has since made her
absence so painful and lonesome. Still I am thankful that I enjoyed
the precious boon as long as I did. Oh, she was always so sweet to
me.

Friday evening called on Erastus Snow's family and found
Elizabeth very comfortable with her little daughter five days old.
Also on Brother Horace Eldridge's folks who were well and attended
the Pollysophical meeting which was very interesting. I read my essay
on the subject of judging one another.

Saturday rode ten miles north and visited Bro. Call's.[7] The
wheat looks well, looks abundant tho in a few patches seemed dried
up for want of water. This is the first north trip I have taken.

Sunday attended meeting in the afternoon and heard Bro. Brigham preach a discourse that was very comforting as well as instruc-
tive to me. Subjects—The Spirit world was right here if we could but
see it; the necessity of having trials and temptations; the necessity
of going through the ordeal of going below all things like unto Jesus
whose birth and life on this earth was of a humiliating character, etc.

June 23rd—Monday—Had a family group taken at [daguerre-
otype] room of Sister Vary, Ida, Nealy and Benny, which consumed
the forenoon. Started from there and made some calls first on Mrs.
Howard where I stayed near an hour. Next on Sister Zina Young

[6] Edward Partridge was the first presiding bishop of the LDS church.
[7] Probably Anson Call.

128

who chaperoned me through Brigham's new house, commencing with the school where Sister Pratt presides.[8] The scholars are all from Bro. Brigham's family and I like her system if she can carry it and advance her pupils in scholastic learning. Went all through the house but a few rooms finished and occupied.[9] A large number of workmen to work. Visited his other house and Sister Maryanna received me very warmly.[10] Tarried about half an hour and had an interview with Brother Brigham who spoke kindly to my little boy and kissed him. Called on Sister Emeline and Sister Wells, also on Bro. Barlow's family and finally found myself at home with a mind full of new thoughts and plans.[11] One of the latter was embroidering. Tuesday after the morning duties started to Sister Leawood's [?] and had a few hours delightful visit and felt strengthened in my purpose of accomplishing something. In the afternoon went down street with Sister Heywood and on our return turned in to Bro. Barlow's and visited there.

July 6th—Sunday—This forenoon attended meeting and heard Brother Brigham preach on the necessity of obeying all the ordinances which will give us light and enable us to know whether we can judge or not, nor can it be expected that persons just coming to the valley ———.

July 20th—Sunday—Four months ago this morning I saw the little tabernacle of my dear Sarepta for the last time, embraced it and saw it covered from my sight. We left the house taking the precious burden to the burial ground, there depositing it in the depth prepared, covering it up and starting from there to this place. For the

[8] Zina Diantha Huntington Smith Young was a sister of Dimick B. and Prescindia. A plural wife of Joseph Smith, Jr., Zina was later married to Brigham Young. She served as the third president of the Relief Society, president of the Silk Association, and vice-president of the National Council of Women. See Jenson, *LDS Biographical Encyclopedia*, 1:697–99. Sister Pratt may have been Keziah Pratt who later had a school at First South and Richards streets.

[9] The Lion House, designed by Truman O. Angell, was built during 1855–56 for the church leader's growing family. The home was several months away from completion, although some of the family were living there. The *Deseret News* of September 24, 1856, announced that the large dwelling was completed. The family's school was in a downstairs room of the Lion House until 1862 when a separate schoolhouse was built for the children. A good description of the rooms Martha may have seen is found in Carter, *Heart Throbs of the West*, 1:234–36.

[10] Martha had stopped at the Beehive House, just east of the new Lion House, and visited with Mary Ann Angell Young. The Beehive House had been completed in 1854. It, too, was designed by Truman O. Angell, Mary Ann's father.

[11] Martha may have visited Emmeline Free Young, a wife of Brigham, and/or Emmeline B. Wells, a wife of Daniel H.

last month I have visited much among my acquaintances. Last Tuesday with Sarepta and Sister Vary spent the afternoon with Bro. Brigham's folks on the Hill. Thursday we all spent the afternoon to Sister Southworth's. Friday I started in the forenoon to make a long contemplated visit to Brother Barney's folks and on the way made some calls, one of which, Sister Haven, I enjoyed.

July 27th—Sunday—Visited the Big Cottonwood canyon which was a very interesting circumstance to me, being the celebration of the 24th. It was a most fitting illustration of the thing to illustrate. It was in my heart to go but I could not think of getting a chance for myself while the rest of the family would remain at home, but Sarepta having arranged a visit to her brothers I felt free to take the first opportunity that presented itself.[12]

This forenoon a Bro. Orrin Smith gave his experiences. It was interesting to me as he went through a Millerite course. Joseph Young followed with the best of instructions to us as a people and then Bro. Brigham followed with a whip on the Bishops. This afternoon we heard from Bro. Townsend who had been to Carson Valley and California.[13] He gave a deplorable account of California and not a very good one of Carson.

August 1st—Attended the Pollysophical party which was very interesting and enjoyed myself very much and had the very great pleasure of dancing with Brigham which did my soul good. Had letters from Mr. Heywood last from Chicago. His health improving all the time.

August 4th—Monday—Commenced to work in the ———— and Sister Woolcot commenced to learn and work at the business. Attended the Agricultural and Mechanical Society meeting and tho few attended the remarks of Bros. Blair and Clements were very interesting.[14] Had a visit to the sugar works, or rather to Sister Smoot which I enjoyed very much.

---

[12] The celebration took place at Brighton in Big Cottonwood Canyon. A large bowery was built for shade. Swings and rafts for use on Silver Lake were designed to entertain the young. The Nauvoo Brass Band, Captain Ballo's Band, and many other musicians provided entertainment and music for dancing that lasted until after midnight. On the Twenty-fourth itself the campers were awakened at five minutes to five with reveille, and at five o'clock two rounds were fired from a cannon. See *Deseret News*, July 30, 1856.

[13] James Foss Townsend had been a missionary companion of Wilford Woodruff in Maine. He reportedly built the first hotel in Utah. See Esshom, *Pioneers and Prominent Men*, p. 352.

[14] The Deseret Agricultural and Manufacturing Society was incorporated on January 17, 1856, by the territorial legislature to promote home industry. See

Sister Vary has been working all the week on the rug designed for the Exhibition and it bids fair to be very fine.

August 9th—Saturday—Attended another A. & M. Meeting. Bro. Brigham was there but did not address the meeting. Heard excellent remarks from Bro. Clements. Pretty well attended.

August 10th—Sunday—Was not well and did not attend the Tabernacle but learned that Bro. Brigham came out in plain terms on home manufacture and the necessity of making our own wearing apparel. Attended ward meeting and Bro. Pack spoke very interesting on home produce and manufacture.

August 8th was the return of dear little Sarepta's birthday but my beautiful daughter has been removed from my care for some reason that I do not yet comprehend.

August 17th—Sabbath—Was addressed by Bro. Whitney and Bro. Brigham in the forenoon and in the afternoon Bro. Merrill and a few remarks from Bro. S———. Home manufacture and the spirit of home manufacture seems much on the increase, although last week's editorial goes to the contrary.[15] Friday evening attended the Pollysophical and was much entertained. I had prepared a subject on home manufacture in rhyme but had not the opportunity of presenting it. Saturday afternoon spent about three hours with Bro. Parley and family where I enjoyed myself much and from there to the Mechanical and Agricultural Society but was very late and only heard some remarks by Bro. Woodruff which were very good and heard a song by Bro. Willis.[16] Our mare Fairner died Wednesday.

August 24th—Sunday—This forenoon Bro. Samuel Wooley gave a report of his mission to Hindustan which was deeply interesting but previous to his speaking Bro. Renny gave a history of himself and Father Cutler of Silver Creek and how he, Father Cutler, was led to apostatize from the Church. After Bro. Renny had con-

Leonard J. Arrington, "The Deseret Agricultural and Manufacturing Society in Pioneer Utah," *Utah Historical Quarterly* 24 (1956): 165–70.

[15] Martha may have been referring to an editorial in the *Deseret News* of August 20, 1856, that posed the problem of locally produced goods such as hats and shoes costing more than the imported items. To be successful, the editorial stated, home manufacturers must produce goods that were better and/or cheaper.

[16] Wilford Woodruff said the society was in its infancy but promising. He showed some soap made by Dr. William France that was superior to the imported article. The apostle said that the ladies could greatly influence home industry by giving it their support. The singer was a W. Willes. See *Deseret News*, August 27, 1856.

cluded his remarks Bro. Kimball stood up and moved and it was seconded and an unanimous vote of the Church that Bro. Renny be accepted as a brother in the Church in full fellowship. Bro. Brigham testified as to his knowledge of his good character and remarked that it was the order to [go] down into the water and be baptized and be confirmed by the laying on of hands.

This evening attended the ward meeting and if ever I heard music from men's voices I heard it tonight from Bro. Blair. He spoke most splendidly.

Eastern mail arrived Friday evening, August 29th and we received three letters from Joseph one of which gave us an account of his Sans ceremony, dismissed from the office of U. S. Marshall. His health was very good and was in good spirits. His business was not in the least settled.[17]

[17] See footnote 15, chapter 11.

APPENDIX

The following letter, written by Martha Spence Heywood to Emmeline Free Young, a wife of Brigham Young, is printed here with the kind permission of the Archives Division, Historical Department, Church of Jesus Christ of Latter-day Saints. It is especially revelatory of Martha's feelings about herself: her lack of domestic skills, her loneliness, and her unusual experiences prior to her marriage.

Nephi Decr 9th [1855] Sunday afternoon

Dear Sister Emeline

How I long to write one good sentimental letter (one of my favorite amusements in past years) But since I've become a wife & mother all sentiment has died away in the realities of life, such as, cooking, washing, waiting on babies, &c, also the continual trafic of borrowing & lending a necessary evil peculiarly adapted to new settlements,—and now that you are actually living in a new settlement even Filmore I will dare to visit with you, through the medium of the pen. But were you yet in the old city of Salt Lake, I wd not think of commiting so great a blunder as to write a love letter to the Lady of the Governor of Utah the youngest but fairest & certainly most virtuous of Uncle Sam's family. I feel lonesome at times even in the proud & boasting city of Nephi, & when a letter arrives from the aforesaid Salt Lake City, it is very interesting.

Now its not for me to say that this letter will be interesting. But if it wiles away a few moments of the dull tedium of domestic affairs (what Felicia Hemans styled "the horrors of dinner ordering." but may be, you cook dinner & wash dishes—possible! Governor's wife washes dishes! Oh my poor nerves!) the endeavor will not be lost.

But to the subject matter. You never was an old maid was you? Well I know you never was, & what of it? Why you know nothing about what I once was, or the path I trod. Well, I learned many things journeying that path, that could not be learnt in any other path, I learned the value of a home, that I now appreciate so highly, ('tho, but three years enjoying this blessing,) the value of belonging to somebody by the years experience of belonging to nobody, and gaining through that Somebody whom we call *Lord,* the rich blessing of children to give tone & exercise to the long treasured up woman's feelings, that many times seemed to burst the vessel that contained them.

I love my home, I dearly love the first & only home I'v had, since I first left my father's house, then in my twenty third year, & experience since then, has proven that I had a good *mother,* whose teachings & precepts comes in play every day of my present life, & whose memory is revered in the deep recesses of my heart. And I want to do by my children, that they may realize in their after years what I have for many years past.

My Mother died in the city of Dublin 14 Febr 1837 I was then in New York City for the second time having crossed the Atlantic Ocean the third time. The event of her death almost crazed me, tho by an unaccountable operation in my mind I left my parents against their will, to come to *America.* But return'd to make reconcilliation with them. I won my father over to an interest in America and he promised me, he would come but my dear mother never manifested a particle of interest in this country but to hate it & died of a broken heart caused by father's preparing to come.

During my visit to the homestead I was an invalid & continually in my mother's company but never could interest her, to converse on any topic relating to America And why? I will tell you, by relating a little of a conversation that occurred between us, "Mother, why do you dislike to hear and talk about America?" Because I hate it! "Will you tell me why you hate it? It has been kind to your children. I know for myself that I have been treated well as a stranger in a strange land." She burst into a flood of tears saying as she rose from her seat & left the room "America has robbed me of my children & therefore do I hate it!" There were three of her children then in this country, and the fourth was determined to return, & I was the sole cause of her severe trouble which ended in her death. The love of America had taken hold of my heart long before I dared to breathe it to any one till a circumstance in my Brother's affairs made a jar in his business department. Then I suggested (with a view to help myself) the advantages of his going to America while young & his family small, he swallowed the bait & talked the thing out in the family, & soon came the desired moment for me to talk also. My father's anger was very severe my mother's more silent but deeper & in a few months I left without *one cent* to defray the expenses of a journey across the Atlantic then Oct 1834 in my 23rd year landed in New York with a debt of $40/—& not a cent to pay the first weeks board. But even in a common boarding house we were regarded (a sister having accompanied me & in the same predicament) as worthy of sympathy & instead of taking our little items of jewelry there was exertions made to find us sewing to pay for our expenses.

Well from that time to this, I have toiled & toiled late & early on acct of poor health I have done it by the hardest being obliged to travel often to recruit my health, did not know how to wash my clothes till I was about thirty years old never cooked or kept house till after I came to Nephi never was a favorite with the multitude but never without one or more true hearted friends, had many offers & expectations to be married but always made it a point to look to the Lord to arrange such affairs for my good. & I firmly believe that I have got the very husband the Lord designed for me. Well are you tired of Sentiment history &c If I was a good housekeeper & had the wherewith I wd prefer making you a good Christmas Cake all dotted over under & through the middle with little black spots & larger brown ones, well "to want to, & can't is hell" so says Bro Brigham

Well I want to be a good housekeeper and I just mean to be one, in due time, I feel my awkardness so keenly, that I make blunders often from that very feeling. I want to improve my character in every respect and the special favor I have recd in the *best men on Earth turning in,* to this humble dwelling & refreshing themselves inspires me with greater zeal to become worthy of such honors. How is life in Filmore. I desire much to pay it a visit while you are there, but have little hopes Best respects to all the good Brethren & Sisters in your company Muff trade progressing slowly Now sister Emeline I have written this by stretches out of two Sundays excuse blunders & please burn it up

Martha S Heywood

INDEX

Alvord, George, 45
Andrews, Sister, 54
Andrews, Mrs., 52
Ashby, Sister, 58

Babbitt, Almon W., secretary of Utah
Territory, 3, 60, 61, 62, 63, 113
Badlam, Miss, 42
Ballantyne, Richard, 85
Ballard, Mrs., 1850 immigrant, 31
Barber, Brother and Sister, 93
Barber, Louisa, 117
Barlow, Israel, 79
Barlow [possibly James M.], 1850
immigrant from Kentucky, 40, 42,
43, 49, 71, 129
Barney, Brother, 1850 immigrant,
14, 129
Bateman, Thomas, 51
Batiste, Nephi Indian, 90, 102
Baxter, Liddy, wife of Zimri H., 72
Baxter, Margaret, wife of Zimri H.,
69, 72
Baxter, Zimri H., early Nephi settler,
65, 66, 67, 68, 70, 72, 73, 81, 100
Bean, George Washington, visits of,
with MSH, 79, 80, 93
Bean, Mrs. George Washington, 79
Bell, Archibald, brother-in-law of
JLH, 96, 120
Beman, Louisa, death of, 53
Benson, Ezra T., LDS apostle, 9, 54,
56, 94, 104
Benson, Mrs., wife of Ezra T., 51, 72
Bennett, Nephi family, 97

Bentley, Brother, Nephi resident, 86,
105
Bentley, Sister, Nephi resident, 86, 116
Bernhisel, John M., delegate to Con-
gress, 63
Billings, Diantha, Manti resident, 68
Billings, Titus, Manti resident, 68, 77
Bigelow, James O., Mona resident, 83,
93
Bigelow, Mrs. James O., Mona resident,
83
Bigler, Amy, 114
Bigler, Jacob G., early settler and
bishop at Nephi, 85, 86, 91, 94, 100,
104, 106, 110, 111
Bigler, Sister, wife of Jacob G., 117
Blair, Mrs. Seth M., 61
Blair, Seth M., U.S. attorney for Utah
Territory, 50, 61, 86, 94, 130, 132
Blodgett, Edgar, brother of Sarepta
Heywood, 46
Blodgett, Theodore, nephew of
Sarepta Heywood, 64, 65, 67, 68, 73
Bordeaux, James P., trading post of, 17
Bradley, George W., early Nephi
settler, 76, 77, 81, 91, 92, 100, 103,
104
Bradley, Sister, wife of George W., 77
Brandebury, Lemuel G., chief justice
of Utah Territory, 61
Broadhead, Brother and Sister, 98, 106
Brosbie, Mrs., 52
Brown, Ebenezer, Draper settler, 64,
124

136

Brown, Gurnsey, Draper settler, 92
Brown, Thomas D., missionary to Indians, 111
Bryan, Charles H., early Nephi settler, 80, 81, 103, 104, 106, 114, 116
Bryan, Sister, wife of Charles H., 77, 79, 80, 83
Buck, Sister, 57
Bullock, Thomas, recorder and clerk, 47, 61, 119
Bullock, Sister, wife of Thomas, 119
Butterfield, Sister, 1850 immigrant, 20, 31, 41, 42, 43, 48, 54, 58, 63

Cahoon, Reynolds, 61
Call, Anson, president of Fillmore settlement, 72, 97, 128
Camp, Brother, Nephi resident, 66, 67
Campbell, Brother, 1850 immigrant, 16–17, 40
Campbell, Mrs., 17
Cannon, Marsena, photographer, 125–26
Carpenter, Brother R., Nephi resident, 100
Carpenter, William H., seventy at Nephi, 104
Carrington, Mrs. Albert, 54
Carter, Mrs., friend of MSH, 62
Cazier, Father, patriarch at Nephi, 100–101
Cazier, Sister, Nephi resident, 77, 79
Chase, Brother, 1850 immigrant, 17
Cholera, 9, 13–14, 63
Clements, Brother, 130, 131
Coleman, Prime T., father-in-law of Joseph Neal Heywood, 5
Condie, Mrs., 1850 immigrant, 19
Cox, Brother, Cottonwood settler, 119
Crosbis, Mrs., 40
Crosby, Sister, 51
Cumming, Brother, son of, discovered murdered men, 86–87
Cunningham, ——, immigrant from Ireland, 40
Cutler, Father, apostasy of, 131

Dana, Charles R., 8
Dana, Mrs. Charles R., 8, 13
Davis, Sister, worked for MSH, 82
Deseret Agricultural and Manufacturing Society (DAMS), 130–31

Eldredge, Horace S., seventies president, 73, 87, 111, 128
Elmore, ——, Nephi resident, 81
Elocution Society, MSH active in, 41, 42, 46
Everett, Brother, Sanpete resident, 71

Farr, Mrs., 57
Fellows, Amelia, household helper for MSH, 93, 100

Felt, Brother, 1850 immigrant, 14, 61
Ferguson, Brother, 38
Ferguson, James, mission of, to Ireland, 99
Foote, Sister, 88, 89
Foote, Timothy Bradley, early Nephi settler, 65, 66, 70, 71, 81, 86, 88, 91, 92, 96, 100, 106, 110
Fort Laramie, Indians at, 17–18
Fosgreen, Brother, 98
Fox, Jesse W., surveyor, 66, 67, 68, 71, 73, 87
Frances, Sister, 80
Fullmer, John S., 3
Fulmer, Mr. and Mrs. Oliver, 52

Gibson, Mrs., friend of MSH, 44
Gifford, Anna, Nephi neighbor of MSH, 70, 75, 97, 100
Gifford, Father, Nephi settler, 65, 66, 67, 71, 72, 94
Gochu, murder victim, 96
Goddard, William, gold miner, 53
Grant, Jedediah M., LDS leader, 3, 54, 107
Green, Nancy, 50
Gunnison Massacre, trial of Indians for, at Nephi, 108
Gustin, Amos, Manti-Nephi resident, 72, 81, 88, 99
Gustin, Mary, 114
Gustin, Sister, 77

Hale, Brother, accompanied MSH on visit, 37
Hale, Mrs. friend of MSH, 33
Hall, John C., friend of MSH from Canada, 7, 39, 44, 46, 51
Hall, Mrs., sister of H. C. Kimball, 8, 35
Hancock, Charles B., Payson bishop, 118, 119
Hancock, Levi W., seventies president, 118–19
Hanks, Ephraim Knowlton, 21, 22
Hanson, Brother, 50
Harrington, Leonard E., American Fork resident, 64–65, 119, 124
Hatch, Jeremiah, Indian farm superintendent, 99, 110, 111
Haven, Sister, 130
Hayes, Mr. and Mrs., friends of MSH, 8, 44, 45, 58, 83, 95
Hendricks, James, 38
Henricks, Sister, helped MSH, 101
Henroid, Gustavus, 103
Heywood, Alice, daughter of JLH and Sarepta, 4, 80, 95–96
Heywood, Benjamin, father of JLH, 3
Heywood family, photograph of, taken, 128
Heywood, Frank, nephew of JLH,

illness and death of, 19, 22–24, 26, 27, 28, 29, 30, 31, 32, 35–37
Heywood, Hannah Rawson, mother of JLH, 3
Heywood, Joseph Leland: activities of, at Nephi, 64, 65–67, 78, 79, 82, 83, 107; biographical data on, 3–6; children of, 4, 63, 75, 80, 82, 95–96, 97, 98, 117–18; death of nephew of, 35; in Dixie, 5; and 1850 immigration, 12, 13, 18–19, 20, 22–23, 24, 27, 29, 30, 31; as hatmaker, 4, 109; health of, 40, 42, 53, 57, 58, 59, 63, 82, 83, 86, 90, 92, 94, 100, 101, 103, 112, 114, 125; and Indians, 97, 100; marriages and sealings of, 32, 45–47, 57, 121; and MSH, 10–11, 33, 34, 41, 76, 77, 80, 89, 114; opposition to leadership of, at Nephi, 91–92, 100, 101, 103, 104–5, 107, 108, 110–11; personality of, 36; proposed mission of, 43, 45, 46, 49, 50, 52; sermons and lectures of, 52, 89, 99, 120; social activities of, 38, 43, 54, 92; travels of, 93, 94, 95, 96, 97, 98, 99, 102; as U.S. marshal, 50, 82, 87 n. 27, 95, 107, 108, 113, 120–21
Heywood, Joseph Neal, son of MSH and JLH, 5, 75, 76, 77, 82, 83, 85, 86, 87, 88, 92, 96, 108, 116, 125
Heywood, Martha Spence: baptism and conversion of, 6, 34; birth of children of, 75, 97, 103–4; cultural activities of, 39, 40, 41, 42, 46, 59; death of, 5; domestic arrangements of, 33, 39, 40–41, 44–45, 80; dreams of, 122–23, 126–27; immigration of, from Ireland, 133–34; and famine in Utah, 124–25; hatmaking of, 4, 9–10, 38, 39–40, 41, 45, 62, 69, 70, 76, 78, 83, 109; health of 40, 41, 44–45, 60, 63, 67, 78, 79, 80, 83, 84, 88, 96, 97, 109, 112, 119, 121, 127; letter of, to Emmeline Free Young, 133–35; location of journal of, 1–2; marriage ordinances of, 47, 57, 121; move of, to Dixie, 5; move of, to Nephi, 64; parents of, 133–34; photograph of, taken, 125–26; poetry of, 29; pregnancy of, 58–59, 62; religious activities of, 7, 44–45; social activities of, 35, 36, 37, 38, 40, 41, 48, 49, 50, 51, 52, 53, 54, 57–58, 60, 61, 63, 77, 78, 79, 83, 84, 85, 88, 89, 97, 98–99, 100, 106, 109, 120, 127, 128–29, 130, 131; as a teacher, 5, 81–82, 83, 84, 99–100, 101, 103, 107, 110; visits of, to Salt Lake City, 79–80, 92–93, 98–99, 109–10, 118–22

Heywood, Mary Bell, fourth wife of JLH, 5–6, 83, 103, 109, 120
Heywood, Sarah Idoo (Ida), daughter of JLH and Sarepta, 63, 80, 82
Heywood, Sarah Symonds (Sister Vary), second wife of JLH, 6, 39, 47, 51, 54, 59, 78, 79, 103, 120, 125, 126, 130, 131
Heywood, Sarepta Marie, daughter of MSH and JLH, 97, 98, 103–4, 112, 116–17, 118
Heywood, Sarepta Marie Blodgett, first wife of JLH: blessing of, 50; children of, 4, 62, 63; death of, 6; and Frank Heywood, 35; and hatmaking, 109; as a housewife, 36; marriage and ordinances of, 3, 47; health of, 53, 54, 59, 60, 83; and MSH, 33–34, 39, 40–41, 45–46, 76, 78, 112; social activities of, 38, 51, 54, 98, 120, 129, 130; visits of, to Nephi, 82, 96, 113, 114
Hodgekiss, Mrs., 51
Hold, Brother, Indian interpreter, 90
Holden, William, and seventies controversy, 110
Hollman, Joseph, U.S. attorney, 108
Homisted, Sister, 53
Horn, Sister, 52, 53
Houston, Brother, 9
Howard, Mrs., 128
Hoyt, Brother, marshal, 95
Humphrey, Smith, 93
Hunt, Jefferson, 52
Hunt, Dr., 108
Hunter, Edward: 1850 immigrant train of, 12, 16, 17, 18, 19, 21, 22, 29, 30, 31; missed Heywood party, 51; at Nephi, 94, 102; as presiding bishop, 56
Hutchinson, Jacob F., 1850 immigrant, 27, 38, 48
Hyde, Orson, LDS apostle, 3, 12, 30, 31, 107
Hyde, Sister, 92

Ivans, Anna, 109
Ives family, 98

Johnson, Benjamin F., 35, 57, 73, 109, 110; letters of, 66, 76, 93; at Nephi, 71, 74, 77–78, 83, 84, 96; and settlement of Santaquin, 67 n. 73
Johnson, Betty, son of, 71
Johnson, Harriet, wife of Benjamin F., 76, 79, 83, 96
Johnson, Joel H., 52, 71
Johnson, Joseph E.: friendship of, with MSH, 5, 11, 34, 38, 39, 44; and hat trade, 9–10, 62; immigration of, to Utah, 12, 59–60
Johnson, Julia, mother of Joseph E., 29, 34 n. 4, 62

Johnson, Mary Anne, wife of
  Benjamin F., 68–69, 70, 71, 72, 73,
  75, 76, 77, 78, 79, 81, 83, 90, 93
Johnson, Melissa, 96
Jones, Dan, 9, 82
Jones, Nathaniel V., 85

Kay, Brother, 48
Kempton, Father, 60, 61
Kendall, George, Nephi resident, 102,
  104, 110, 111
Kimball, Amanda, wife of Heber C.,
  94
Kimball, Ann Alice Gheen, wife of
  Heber C., 51, 109
Kimball, Christeen Golden, wife of
  Heber C., 51, 109
Kimball, Ellen Sanders, wife of Heber
  C., 51
Kimball, Franey (Frances Swan), wife
  of Heber C., 33, 42
Kimball, Heber C., 54, 73, 79, 99,
  132; and Elocution Society, 46;
  health of, 41; and MSH, 33, 38, 39,
  47; Nephi visits of, 93, 101, 102,
  109, 114; preaching and lectures of,
  37, 48, 54, 59, 61, 99, 107, 127
Kimball, Hiram, 95
Kimball, Laura Pitkin, wife of Heber
  C., 51
Kimball, Lucy Walker, wife of Heber
  C., 101, 102
Kimball, Maryanne, divorce of, from
  Heber C., 124
Kimball, Mary Ann Shefflin, wife of
  Heber C., 51, 79
Kimball, Mrs. Heber C. (unidentified
  wives), 33, 41, 68
Kimball, Mrs. Hiram, 120
Kimball, Oliver, brother-in-law of
  JLH, 3
Kimball, Prescindia Huntington, wife
  of Heber C., 121
Kimball, Ruth Reese, wife of Heber
  C., 62
Kimball, Sarah Lawrence, wife of
  Heber C., 24–25, 48
Kimball, Vilate, wife of Heber C.,
  47, 73, 99
Kinkead, Charles A., pioneer merchant,
  63
Kinney, John F., chief justice of Utah
  Territory, 108
Klingensmith, Philip, Manti resident,
  69
Knapp, Mrs., 8
Knowlton, Brother, 58

Leamond, Mrs., 83
Lebanon, David, 119
Lee, Ezekiel, physician, 59
Lee, John D., 72
Leonard, Brother, 53

Leonard, Sister, 55
Leroy, Julia, 101
Lewens, Mr. and Mrs., 37
Lewens, Thomas, friend of MSH, 7,
  10, 11, 21, 30, 44, 52, 60, 122
Lion House, completion of, 129
Livingston, James Monroe, pioneer
  merchant, 59, 61, 63
Llingerline, ———, accused horse
  thief, 94
Loetzky, Mrs., 46
Love, Andrew, Mona resident, 83,
  107, 110
Love, Sister Andrew, Mona resident, 79
Lyman, Amasa M., 34, 51
Lynch, Patrick, 120

MacDougal, Margaret, cholera victim,
  13
McKenna, Mr., 10
McLellan, Brother, Payson resident,
  64, 65
McPherson, Captain, 1850 immigrant,
  20
Major, ———, 60
Manning, Sister, 1850 immigrant, 27
May, William, murderer, 96
Meeks, Lizzy, 112
Meeks, William, opposition to, as
  president of Nephi seventies, 110–11
Mercer, Brother, American Fork
  resident, 80
Merrill, Brother, friend of Heywoods,
  109, 120, 124–25, 131
Miller, Josiah, 66, 67; and JLH
  leadership controversy, 92, 103, 104,
  objected to teacher's salary, 81
Morley, Isaac, 69, 77, 84, 85;
  blessings given by, 78, 89; Indians
  killed on orders of, 97; sermon of, 88
Morley, Mrs. Isaac, 72, 84
Mount Nebo Literary Association, 89,
  90
Murray, Fanny, sister of Brigham
  Young, 29, 35, 50
Murray, Mr., 35

Nephi: celebrations at, 84, 107–8;
  cultural life of, 89, 90; description
  of, 76; election at, 100; fort at, 86,
  98, 99, 100, 101, 102, 107 n. 4;
  Indian farm at, 99, 101; settlement
  and growth of, 65–67, 84, 86, 98
Noble, Mary Beman, 53
Noble, Mrs., 68
Nobles, Brother, 79
Nobles, Sister, 79
Nugent, Brother, Nephi resident, 100

Ollerton, Fay, and MSH journal, 1

Pace, James, Payson settler, 79
Pack, ———, ball at home of, 42

Pack, Brother, 98, 131
Pack, Mrs., 49
Pack, Mother, sang in tongues, 50
Pack, Ruth Mosher, interpreted tongues, 50
Partridge, Edward, revelation concerning, 127–28
Patten, Brother, 71
Peck, Brother, prayer meeting at home of, 53
Perkins, Brother, death of, 37
Perkins, Sister, death of, 37
Petit, Nephi Indian, 89
Pine, Sister, Springville resident, 65
Pitt, William, 1850 immigrant, 27
Polysophical Society, 126, 127, 128, 130
Pooro, Nephi Indian, 90
Pratt, Brother, 54
Pratt, Mrs. Orson, 109
Pratt, Orson, mission of, 94–95, 99
Pratt, Parley P., 37, 101; sermons of, 48, 49, 84; social activities of, 49, 131; toll road of, 56–57
Pratt, Phebe, wife of Parley P., 84
Pratt, Sister, teacher, 129

Randall, Sister, spoke in tongues, 50
Redfield, Harlow, Provo resident, 119
Reese, Colonel, merchant, 13
Renny, Brother, apostasy and rebaptism of, 131–32
Rich, Charles C., 54
Richards, Franklin D., 10, 87, 88
Richards, Silas, Little Cottonwood bishop, 119
Richards, Susanna, 62
Richards, Willard, 60
Richardson, Brother, 1850 immigrant, 23
Ried, Eliza, 49
Rin, Elder, 1850 immigrant, 31
Rist, Brother, 99
Robinson, Lewis, 94
Rockwell, Merrill, 1850 immigrant, 19
Rockwood, Albert P., seventies president, 111
Rogus, Freeman, New York Mormon, 8
Rosad, Mrs., triplets born to, 57
Rose, Brother and Sister, 98

Sackett, Mr. and Mrs., New Yorkers, 8, 9
Salt Lake Tabernacle (old), 80
Sanderson, Maj. W. F., commander at Fort Laramie, 18
Sargeant, Brother, cholera victim, 13–14
Sawyer, Elder, 45
Savage, Miss, 40
Savage, Sister, 51
Scriggins, Mary Anne, worked for MSH, 106, 107

Segar, Brother, 1850 immigrant, 17
Sen, Sister, 77
Sherman, Susan, worked for MSH, 112, 113
Sherwood, Henry G., San Bernardino settler, 84
Shumway, Brother, Payson resident, 93
Shumway, Mary, teacher, 77
Siler, Brother, 100
Sindy, Mrs., 63
Sly, James Calvin: and JLH leadership controversy, 91, 92, 94; mission of, 99
Smith, Bathsheba, wife of George A., 94
Smith, Brother, 127
Smith, Candace, Nephi teacher, 79, 80, 88, 89
Smith, George A.: at bishops' meeting, 37; and MSH, 34, 39, 110; Provo home of, 92; sermons of, 35, 37, 38, 85; travels of, 73, 79, 94, 96
Smith, John, 34, 125
Smith, John C. L., Parowan settler, 70–71
Smith, Joseph, Jr., at baptism of JLH, 3
Smith, Lucy, wife of George A., 92, 125
Smith, Orrin, 130
Smith, Sarah, death of, 125
Smithy, Doctor, homeopath, 15
Smoot, Abraham O.: 1850 wagon train of, 18, 20, 22; at Little Cottonwood, 64
Snider, Mrs., 62
Snow, Barnard, 122
Snow, Brother, 62
Snow, Eliza R., and MSH, 35, 120
Snow, Erastus, 119, 128; as missionary, 10, 99; sermons of, 87, 88, 118
Snow, Lorenzo, 10
Snow, Mother, 61
Snow, Mr. and Mrs. William, 52
Snow, Mrs. Zerubbabel, 79
Snow, Sister Erastus (Artimesia Beman), 53
Snow, Willard, 52
Snow, William, friend of MSH, 36, 38, 59
Snow, Zerubbabel, associate justice of Utah Territory, 63, 79, 85, 93
Sonsin, Sister, 79
Southworth, Sister, 130
Spence, Andrew, brother of MSH, 45
Spence, Anna Maria, sister of MSH, 45
Spence, Ellen, sister of MSH, 45
Spencer, Brother, Nephi teacher, 88
Spencer, George, 104, 112
Spencer, Orson, 50, 99
Sperry, Josephine, 97
Sprague, Dr. Samuel Linzey, physician attending Frank Heywood, 36

Steptoe, Edward Jenner, commanded troops sent to investigate Gunnison Massacre, 108
Stevens, Brother, 11
Stewart, Andrew Jackson, 118
Stewart, Brother, 96
Stiles, George P., associate justice of Utah Territory, 107
Stocking, Brother, 52
Stout, Hosea, 107, 120
Strange, Sarah, dressmaker, 41
Stratton, Joseph A., 1850 immigrant, 20, 21, 22
Stratton, Mrs., 57
Stratton, Sister, 52, 53
Streper, Sister, 98
Stringam, Mrs., 57
Strong, Alvah, friend of MSH, 7
Strong, Mrs. Alvah, friend of MSH, 8, 11, 35, 44, 58, 83

Taylor, John, 10, 93; blessed MSH, 14, 33; preaching of, 92, 102
Taylor, Leonora, wife of John, 93, 94
Taylor, Mrs. John, 51
Taylor, Sister, 52, 53
Therman, Mrs., 62
Towndrows, Joseph, mail carrier, 78, 96
Townsend, Brother, 130
Tyrrel, Sister, 51

Udell, Brother, 84

Vary, Mrs. or Sister. *See* Heywood, Sarah Symonds
Vaughan, ———, accused horse thief, 95
Vickers, Brother, English immigrant, 84
Vickers, Sister John, 104, 118

Walker, Chief, 41, 100, 102
Walker War, 97–98
Walton, ———, married ex-wife of Heber C. Kimball, 124
Washburn, Brother, 71
Weldon, Sister, 88
Wells, Daniel H., 83
Wells, Sister, 129
Wheelock, Cyrus H., 94
Whipple, Edson, 1850 immigrant, 21
White, David, Canadian Mormon, 7
White, Mr., 10, 11, 44
Whitesides, Mrs., 11
Whitney, Brother, 131
Whitney, Newel K., death of, 56
Whitney, Sister, 120
Willes, W., singer, 131

Winallis, Brother, 42
Winds, Sister, wife of William Snow, 36
Woodruff, Wilford: at bishops' meeting, 37; at DAMS meeting, 131; 1850 immigrant company of, 20, 21, 22, 24, 28–29
Woolcott, R. W., death of, 125
Woolcot, Sister, 130
Woolley, Anne, wife of Edwin D., 51
Woolley, Edwin D., 51; purchasing mission of, 4, 10; record of 1850 immigrant company of, 12–32; store of, 38
Woolley, John, wedding of, 54–55
Woolley, Samuel A., Hindustan mission of, 85, 131
Woolf, John A., acting seventies president at Nephi, 110
Woolf, William, 114
Wright, Brother, 107, 113
Wright, Sister, 113

Young, Brigham, 50, 86, 95, 125, 132; and 1850 immigration, 21, 29; and Fillmore settlement, 72–73; and Heywoods, 38, 39–40, 46–47; and Nephi, 66, 93, 94, 101–2, 106, 108–9, 110, 111, 113–14; preaching of, 35, 37–38, 48, 51, 52, 53, 54, 56, 58, 59, 61, 80, 101, 120, 122, 127–28, 129, 130, 131; social and cultural activities of, 42, 54, 130, 131; threat against, 94
Young, Emily Partridge, wife of Brigham, 106
Young, Emmeline Free, 101; letter to, from MSH, 133–35
Young, Harriet, wife of Gurnsey Brown, 92
Young, Joseph: 1850 immigrant company of, 20; and MSH, 36; at Nephi, 101; preaching of, 59, 127, 130; sawmill of, 11; and seventies controversy at Nephi, 110, 111
Young, Lorenzo Dow, 101
Young, Margaret Pierce, wife of Brigham, 93
Young, Mrs. Joseph, 36, 58
Young, Persis Goodall, wife of Lorenzo Dow, 29
Young, Phineas, 101
Young, Sister, 77
Young, Vilate, wife of Heber C. Kimball, 93, 94
Young, Zina D. Huntington, wife of Brigham, 109, 129
Youth's Theatrical Society, 40